M000275198

# Physics

## What do plants need to grow?

The plant on the right in the photograph has been in the dark for two weeks. The plant on the left was grown in the light.

*This plant was grown in the light.*

*This plant was grown in the dark.*

**?**

**1** Which of these things do you think plants need to grow well?

> frost    healthy leaves
> healthy roots
> healthy stems    light
> rabbits    snow
> warmth    water

**P**

Look at the photograph of the plants above.
- Write a list of words which describe the plant on the right.
- What do you think will happen if this plant is put in the light for a few weeks? Make a **prediction**.

**C**

In an investigation some little plants were placed in different areas for two weeks.

*These are the little plants at the beginning of the investigation.*

*Plant 1 was not watered and was left in the light.*

*Plant 2 was watered and left in the light.*

*Plant 3 was watered and left in the dark.*

- Which plant was the healthiest after two weeks?
- This investigation shows that two things are needed for a plant to grow well. What are these two things? Why do you think this?

Plants grow by making new materials that are used to make new leaves, stems and roots. Plants make these new materials from water and air. The new materials are made in the leaves but only when there is light. Plants also need to be warm to grow.

## Nutrients

Gardeners put **fertilisers** on their soil to help plants to grow. The pictures show two labels, one from a packet of fertiliser and one from a plant.

Fertilisers contain **nutrients** which plants need in small amounts to help them grow well. Plants take in nutrients through their roots. Soil contains nutrients (and water) but you don't need soil to grow plants. The plants in the picture below are growing in water instead of soil. Nutrients have been added to the water.

*These plants are growing in water with nutrients added to it. Plants take in nutrients through their roots.*

2 a How does a plant get the water it needs?
  b Apart from water, what other substance does a plant need to be able to make new materials? (*Hint*: Light is not a substance.)
3 Why do plants need light?

**SupaGrow Plant Fertiliser**

Just feed SupaGrow Plant fertiliser to your plants once a fortnight and watch your plants grow and grow! SupaGrow plant fertiliser contains all the nutrients that your plants need.

*Clematis arabella*

**Height**: 180 cm
**Position**: Sun or shade.
**Planting**: Stand this container in water for 15 minutes and then plant in a large hole.
**Feeding**: Use fertiliser in spring and again in early summer.

4 a Why do plants need nutrients?
  b How do plants take in the nutrients they need?
5 a How many times each year should a gardener put extra nutrients on *Clematis* plants?
  b What do you think is the advantage of giving the plants extra nutrients?
6 Write down two differences between the way you get materials that you need to grow and the way that plants get them.

## You should know...

- Plants need light to make new materials.
- Plants make new materials using air and water.
- Plants also need nutrients and warmth to grow well.
- Water and nutrients get into a plant through its roots.

## How do we know that plants use air and water to make food?

Aristotle (384–322 BCE) was a Greek scientist who thought that plants ate soil and sucked it up through their roots. Most people believed this until the 17th century.

In the 17th century, a scientist called Jan van Helmont (1579–1644) tested Aristotle's theory. He measured the masses of a small tree and some soil in a pot. He planted the tree and watered it for five years.

In van Helmont's experiment the mass of the soil did not go down much but the mass of the tree went up a lot. This showed that Aristotle's theory was wrong. Van Helmont suggested that the tree got all its food from water.

In 1782, Jean Senebier (1742–1809) showed that plants need carbon dioxide gas from the air and suggested that plants only use this gas to make food.

In 1804, Nicholas de Saussure (1767–1845) did van Helmont's experiment again, but he carefully measured the amounts of carbon dioxide and water he gave to the plant. He showed that both carbon dioxide and water are needed.

*A statue of Aristotle.*

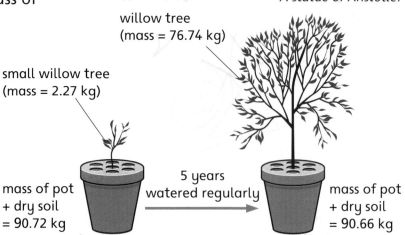

*Van Helmont's experiment.*

willow tree (mass = 76.74 kg)

small willow tree (mass = 2.27 kg)

mass of pot + dry soil = 90.72 kg

5 years watered regularly

mass of pot + dry soil = 90.66 kg

1 a How much mass did van Helmont's tree gain?
   b In van Helmont's experiment, how much mass did the soil lose?
   c Why does this prove that Aristotle was wrong?
   d Why do you think the soil lost some mass?
2 What was Jean Senebier's theory?
3 What did Nicholas de Saussure's experiment show?

## How do we tell the difference between living things?

Plants in garden centres all have labels to say what they are. The people who work in garden centres need to tell the difference between plants so they can put the right labels on them.

These two roses have the same colour flowers, but rose A has narrower, smoother leaves than rose B. Things like flower colour, flower shape and leaf shape are all good ways of telling the difference between plants.

Rose A.

Rose B.

**?**
1  List the differences between these two plants.

Holly.  Silver birch.

You can tell animals apart by looking at things like colour, what the body is covered with and the number of legs. Sometimes differences are hard to spot. Many people can't tell the difference between a butterfly and a moth, but moths have much hairier bodies.

**?**
2  Write down two differences between a moth and a butterfly.
3  a  What differences can you see between the frog and the moth?

Frog.  Toad.

   b  What differences can you see between the frog and the toad?
4  What job might someone have if they needed:
   a  to tell plants apart
   b  to tell animals apart?

antennae

Butterfly (left).  Moth.

**You should know...**

- We can tell living things apart by looking at their differences.

# What is a key and how is it used?

We can look at the differences between living things to find out their names. We can use a **key** to help us do this.

This key is about some birds. We can use it to find out the name of the bird in the picture below. We start at the top and ask the questions as we go down the key.

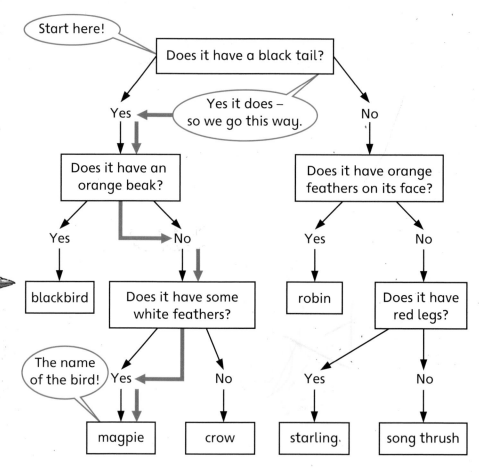

Start here!

Does it have a black tail?

Yes it does – so we go this way.

Yes

No

Does it have an orange beak?

Does it have orange feathers on its face?

Yes

No

Yes

No

blackbird

Does it have some white feathers?

robin

Does it have red legs?

The name of the bird!

Yes

No

Yes

No

magpie

crow

starling

song thrush

---

**?**

**1** Use the key to find out the names of these birds.

A

B

**2** Look at the key and answer these questions.
  **a** What colour beak does a blackbird have?
  **b** Does a song thrush have red legs?
  **c** Does a song thrush have a black tail?

## You should know...

• How to use a key.

## What are the differences between plants growing in different places?

Plants of the same type may look different if they are growing in different places. The photographs show plantain plants growing in a lawn and in a wood.

**?**

**1** Write down a list of differences between the two plantain plants.

> I think we should measure the plants with a ruler.

> I think the sizes of the stems will be different.

> I think dandelions in long grass will have bigger flowers.

> I think the sizes of the leaves will be different.

> I don't think there will be any difference between daisies growing in short and long grass.

**P**

You are going to investigate whether a plant looks different when growing in short or long grass.
- What type of plant will you investigate?
- What differences will you look for?
- How many of the plants will you look at?
- Will you need any apparatus to do your investigation? If so, what apparatus will you need? How will you use it?
- What will you do to stay safe when you do your investigation?

9

## How do animals and plants help each other?

Many animals need plants for food but they also use plants in other ways. Some animals can make their homes from plants, and some animals find shade beneath them on hot days.

 **1** List three ways in which animals use plants.

*Many birds build their nests in trees.*

*This deer is using the trees for shade.*

## Plants depend on animals

Plants also need animals. Animal droppings make a useful fertiliser for plants and many animals help to **disperse** seeds. They can also help to spread pollen.

 **2** List two ways in which plants depend on animals.

*This field used to have cows in it. The grass is growing better where there are cowpats!*

*Goosegrass fruits get stuck to animal fur and are carried long distances before being scraped off.*

## Habitats

The place where something lives is called a **habitat**. For example, bluebells live in a woodland habitat and worms live in an underground habitat. Each living thing is suited to its habitat.

Bluebells have leaves in spring, before the trees above them open their leaves. This means that the bluebells can get lots of sunlight to make food. They store this food in an underground bulb. When the trees open their leaves the bluebell plants die but enough food is stored in the bulbs for the next year. Bluebells are suited to living in a woodland habitat.

The photograph shows some ways in which an earthworm is suited to living in an underground habitat.

**?**

3 What is a habitat?
4 Describe three ways in which an earthworm is suited to where it lives.
5 Squirrels have long claws which are good for gripping. How are squirrels suited to living in woods?

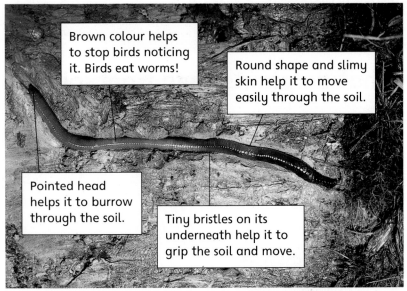

Brown colour helps to stop birds noticing it. Birds eat worms!

Round shape and slimy skin help it to move easily through the soil.

Pointed head helps it to burrow through the soil.

Tiny bristles on its underneath help it to grip the soil and move.

*An earthworm is suited to living in an underground habitat.*

## Food chains

A **food chain** shows what eats what in a habitat.

oak tree → snail → thrush → sparrowhawk

Each arrow means 'is eaten by'.

Food chains always start with something that produces its own food. These things are called **producers**. Plants are producers. Animals eat, or consume, other living things and so they are called **consumers**.

**?**

6 What is a producer?
7 What do the arrows in a food chain mean?
8 In the food chain above, name:
   a a producer
   b a consumer.
9 Mr Chadwick went into his garden to find that slugs had eaten his lettuces. Just then he noticed a large bird. 'A falcon' he thought. 'It's a beautiful bird but it will eat the thrushes which I need to kill my slugs!' Draw a food chain for the garden.

### You should know...

- How animals and plants help each other.
- A habitat is where something lives.
- A food chain shows what eats what in a habitat.

## What do plants need from soil?

When you go to a garden centre, all the plants have labels on them. These labels tell you what the plant is and how to look after it.

> **Hosta**
> *Wide brim*
>
> 🏆 RHS Award of Golden Merit. This hardy perennial bears large blue-green leaves with wide, creamy margins. Lavender-blue flowers open in summer. Excellent for ground cover.
>
> **Height and spread** 45 cm × 60 cm (18 in × 24 in).
>
> **Position** Prefers well-drained soil in shade or partial shade.

> **Clematis**
> *Liberation*™
> *'Evifive'*
>
> Large flowers of pink with cerise bars are freely borne in both early and late summer/early autumn by this vigorous deciduous climber.
>
> **Height** 240–300 cm (8–10 ft).
>
> **Position** Prefers moist but not waterlogged soil. West or east facing aspects with shade at base of plant.

**?**

1 Look at the plant labels.
   a Which plant prefers more shade?
   b Which plant prefers wetter soil?
   c Why do you think it is important for gardeners to have this information?

## Roots

Plants use their roots to take in water and nutrients from the soil. Different plants have different shaped roots.

Some roots go deep into the ground to find water. Other roots spread out over a large area to collect the water that falls as rain.

Roots also help to keep a plant in the ground and stop it falling over. Sometimes, though, a strong wind can break the roots and the plants fall over.

**!** This sort of fig tree, growing in South Africa, has the deepest roots in the world. They go down 120 m!

2 Look at this drawing of a cactus and its roots. How do the roots of the cactus allow it to get enough water in the desert?

3 Make a drawing of a carrot plant growing in soil. Put arrows on your drawing to show how water and nutrients get into the carrot plant.

4 Roots take in nutrients. Name two other things they do for plants.

## Soils

Different plants are suited to different types of soil. Most plants grow best in soils that have lots of nutrients and hold water, but do not become muddy.

Garden soils hold water but don't get muddy. They contain lots of nutrients.

Sandy soils are crumbly and do not have many nutrients. Water runs quickly through the soil because there are lots of air spaces.

Chalky soils are crumbly and do not have many nutrients. Water runs quickly through the soil.

Woodland soils have many nutrients. Water runs quite quickly through the soil.

Clay soils crack when they are dry and become sticky and muddy when they are wet. They hold a lot of water.

How would you observe different soils closely?
- What apparatus would you use?
- What observations would you make?

5 Describe two differences between the woodland soil and the chalky soil.

6 Which soil do you think would be best for plant roots to hold a plant in place? Explain your answer.

7 Which soil do you think would be best for an earthworm? Explain your answer.

### You should know...

- Different plants are suited to different conditions.
- Roots take in water and nutrients, and help to hold the plant in place.
- There are many different types of soil.

13

## How are food chains in a pond like other food chains?

The animals and plants that live in a pond habitat are all suited to living around or under the water. For example, fish have **gills** that allow them to breathe underwater. Pond weeds have leaves near the surface of the water so that the plants get enough light to make their own food.

Fish have fins so that they can swim well.

stickleback

Gills allow fish to breathe underwater.

> 1 **a** Give two ways in which fish are suited to living in a pond habitat.
> **b** How is pond weed suited to living in a pond?
> 2 Name one producer in the pond.

### Herbivores and carnivores

Water fleas are common in ponds. They eat very tiny plants called algae (pronounced '*al-gee*' or '*al-jee*'). Animals that eat only plants are called **herbivores**.

Many animals eat other animals. For example, stickleback fish eat water fleas. Animals that eat other animals are called **carnivores**.

*Water fleas (shown 10 times bigger than real life).*

> 3 Pikes are big fish that eat sticklebacks. Are pikes carnivores or herbivores?
> 4 Name two producers from a pond habitat.
> 5 Draw a food chain using the living things you have read about so far on this page.

### Predators and prey

An animal that eats another animal is a **predator** and what it eats is called its **prey**. So, a stickleback is a predator of water fleas and water fleas are its prey.

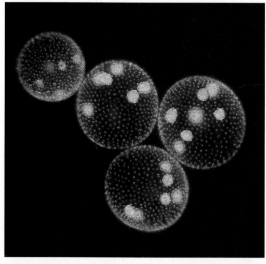

*Algae (shown 40 times bigger than real life).*

## Looking at ponds

You can find out what is living in a pond by **pond dipping**. You put a net into the pond and sweep it through the water. You then empty the net into a bucket of water and look at what you have got.

*Pond dipping.*

## Comparing food chains

Food chains in ponds are similar to all other food chains – they just have different plants and animals. All food chains have producers, consumers, predators, prey, herbivores and carnivores. *All* the animals in any food chain depend on having a producer at the start of the food chain, otherwise there would be no food!

### You should know...

- What herbivores and carnivores are.
- What predators and prey are.

**6** Look at the photograph.
  **a** Which of the animals is the predator?
  **b** Which of the animals is the prey?
  **c** Look carefully at the bird, which is called a heron. How is it suited to living by ponds? Explain your answer.

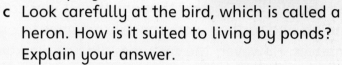

**7** Which of these words describe a stickleback?

| | | |
|---|---|---|
| carnivore | consumer | herbivore |
| predator | prey | producer |

**0**

Jack thinks that the same animals will be found in all parts of a pond. Sam thinks that different animals will be found in different parts. They did some pond dipping to try to find out. Here are the animals they found.

*Animals found near the top of the pond.*

*Animals found at the bottom of the pond.*

- Who was right?
- How do you know this?

**?**

**8** Here are two food chains.

pond weed → common pond snail → common toad → heron

wood anemone → shield bug → badger
  **a** List all the predators in the food chains.
  **b** List all the herbivores in the food chains.
  **c** List all the consumers in the food chains.

## What are micro-organisms?

In the 17th century, thousands of people died of a disease called the plague. Doctors thought that it was caused by smelly air and so they wore special costumes to protect themselves. However, the costumes did not work very well.

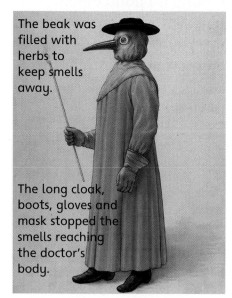

The beak was filled with herbs to keep smells away.

The long cloak, boots, gloves and mask stopped the smells reaching the doctor's body.

*Doctors wore costumes to try to stop them getting the plague.*

**?** 1 How was a doctor's plague costume meant to work?

Today we know that the plague is caused by a **micro-organism** (or **microbe**). Micro-organisms are tiny living things that can only be seen with a **microscope**. The micro-organisms that cause diseases are often called **germs**, but this is not a scientific word.

*Microscopes were invented in about 1590. You can use them to see micro-organisms.*

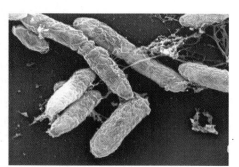

**?** 2 What is a micro-organism?

*This is the micro-organism that causes the plague. It is shown here 6000 times bigger than real life.*

A Roman scientist, Marcus Varro (116–29 BCE), first suggested that tiny living things caused diseases but he had no evidence. So, until the 19th century, people believed that diseases were caused by all sorts of strange things, including the gods and the stars!

**?** 3 Why did Marcus Varro have no evidence for how he thought diseases were caused?
4 This is a pomander. People in the 17th century used to fill them with herbs and carry them around. Why do you think they did this?

**!** People used to think that influenza (or flu) was caused by the influence of the stars. Influenza is Italian for 'influence'.

### You should know...

- Micro-organisms are tiny living things.
- Some micro-organisms can cause diseases.

## How were germs discovered?

Micro-organisms were first seen by a Dutch scientist called Anton van Leeuwenhoek (1632–1723). It was nearly two hundred years later that micro-organisms were found to cause diseases.

In the 19th century, the French silk industry was in trouble because the silkworms were getting a disease. In 1865, a scientist called Antoine Béchamp (1816–1908) discovered rod-shaped micro-organisms in the silkworms with the disease. He said that these micro-organisms caused the disease, but another scientist, Louis Pasteur, did not believe him.

You look through the hole on this side.

What you want to look at goes on this point.

*Leeuwenhoek's simple microscope.*

1 What was Béchamp's theory?

Pasteur then did an experiment. He took two sets of healthy silkworms. He fed the first set with mulberry leaves rubbed with the remains of silkworms with the disease. He fed the second set with mulberry leaves rubbed with the remains of healthy silkworms. Only the first set of silkworms got the disease. The rod-shaped micro-organisms were found in their bodies but not in the bodies of the healthy caterpillars. So, Béchamp had been right but Pasteur had found the **evidence** that Béchamp's theory was true.

*Caterpillars called silkworms make silk.*

2 Did Pasteur do a fair test? Explain your answer.
3 What instrument do you think Pasteur and Béchamp used to see micro-organisms?

### You should know...

- Evidence is needed to show that a theory is right.

*Louis Pasteur (1822–1895).*

# What diseases are caused by micro-organisms?

Many diseases are caused by micro-organisms but some are not. For example, scurvy is a disease caused by a lack of vitamin C in your diet.

There are three main types of micro-organisms: **viruses**, **bacteria** and some **fungi**.

## Viruses

Viruses cause diseases like colds, flu and chicken pox. You can easily catch diseases like these from other people when they sneeze into the air. You should always try to sneeze into a handkerchief to avoid spreading diseases.

## Bacteria

Bacteria cause diseases like food poisoning and impetigo (pronounced 'im-pet-I-go'). They also cause conditions like boils and **tooth decay**.

Bacteria in your mouth feed on sugar in your food. They make substances called acids that can make holes in your teeth **(tooth decay)**. The bacteria can also damage your gums and cause **gum disease**, which can make your teeth fall out. You need to brush your teeth twice a day to remove the bacteria from your teeth.

## Fungi

Only some fungi are micro-organisms. These can cause conditions like athlete's foot.

*Athlete's foot causes the skin between your toes to get itchy and start to peel off.*

1 **a** Name a human disease caused by micro-organisms.
  **b** Name a human disease not caused by micro-organisms.

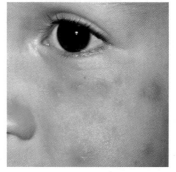
*If you have chicken pox you feel hot and have spots with yellow tops on them.*

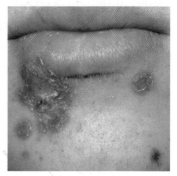
*If you have impetigo you feel hot and get blisters that leave yellow scabs.*

2 Why should you brush your teeth regularly?
3 Name a disease caused by a virus.
4 Imagine you have chicken pox. Write a letter to your teacher to explain why you can't come to school. Include a description of what is wrong with you.
5 Find out which micro-organisms these people discovered: Edwin Klebs, Robert Koch, Luc Montagnier, Alexandre Yersin. Write down where you get your information from.

### You should know...

- Some diseases and conditions caused by micro-organisms.

## What are vaccinations?

People often have injections, called **vaccinations**, to stop them getting diseases.

When you are vaccinated you are injected with a **vaccine**. A vaccine contains dead or weak forms of the micro-organism that causes a disease. The vaccine will not give you the disease, but your body makes chemicals called **antibodies** to destroy the micro-organisms in the vaccine. These antibodies then stay in your body, often for the rest of your life. If the real, nasty micro-organism gets inside you, the antibodies are ready to destroy them.

You need a different type of antibody to destroy each type of micro-organism, which is why you need to have different vaccines for different diseases.

| Age | Vaccine given |
|---|---|
| 2–4 months | diphtheria, whooping cough, polio, tetanus |
| 1–2 years | measles, mumps, rubella |
| 3–5 years | diphtheria, tetanus, polio |
| 10–14 years | rubella (given to girls if they have not already had the vaccine) |
| 13 years | tuberculosis |

Vaccinations were invented by Edward Jenner (1749–1823).

*The ages when people are vaccinated against certain diseases. Some vaccines need to be given more than once to make sure that they work.*

You only get some diseases once because of antibodies. For example, if you are ill with measles, your body makes antibodies to destroy the measles viruses. After a few days you start to get better because the antibodies have now been made. If measles viruses get into you again, the antibodies are already there to destroy them. However, diseases like colds are caused by many different viruses so you will always get these diseases!

**?**

1 What is a vaccination?
2 Which vaccinations do you only need to have once?
3 Explain why you can only get mumps once.
4 Find out why only girls are given the rubella vaccine when they are about 12 years old.

## How does decay occur?

This food has gone mouldy! **Mould** is a micro-organism but there is so much of it here that you can see it.

In 1928, Alexander Fleming (1881–1955) found a medicine that can kill bacteria. He got it from mould!

As well as mould, there are many other micro-organisms that you cannot see, growing and reproducing on the food. The micro-organisms feed on the food and turn it into other things, and this is called **decay**. This happens fastest when it is warm and damp. The micro-organisms can also make you very ill with **food poisoning**.

## Food safety

Foods like meat contain micro-organisms, which can cause food poisoning, but they are killed by cooking. You should never use a knife that has been used to cut raw meat to cut cooked meat because micro-organisms will get carried onto the cooked meat.

### You should know...

• Micro-organisms cause decay and can cause food poisoning.

What factors might affect how quickly mould grows?
• Name some places you could leave the food to investigate these factors.

1 What does mouldy food look like?
2 What is decay?
3 How do you think you get food poisoning?

*Environmental health officers inspect restaurant kitchens to make sure that food is being prepared safely.*

4 Why should meat be properly cooked?
5 Why do you think many fresh foods are kept in a fridge?
6 Find out what happens if you get food poisoning.

## How can decay be useful?

Dead things, like leaves, don't pile up in nature but disappear because micro-organisms feed on them. This is useful because the dead things contain substances called **nutrients**, which plants need to grow. When the dead things decay, the nutrients go into the soil.

## Compost heaps

Gardeners often put vegetable peelings, leaves and grass clippings on a **compost heap**. Eventually the dead things decay to make **compost**, which gardeners put on the soil.

**1** What would happen if dead things did not decay in nature?
**2** What are nutrients?

Dead things are added to the top of the compost heap.

After a while compost can be taken from the bottom of the heap.

**C**

What evidence is there in these photographs that mould is a living thing?

**3** Why do gardeners put compost on their gardens?

## Landfill sites

Many manufactured things, like plastic and glass, don't decay and can litter the environment. When we throw them away, they are dumped in huge **landfill sites**.

**4** Name two things which:
  **a** will decay    **b** will not decay.
**5** Suggest one way we could reduce the size of landfill sites.

### You should know...

- The decay of dead things puts nutrients into the soil.
- Many manufactured things do not decay.

# Investigating yeast

## What is needed to keep yeast alive?

Although some micro-organisms make food decay, other micro-organisms help us to make food. **Yeast** is a type of fungus that is used to make most types of bread. It feeds on sugar in the bread mixture (called dough) and makes bubbles of a gas called carbon dioxide. These bubbles make the bread dough rise and it is then baked.

To make this bread, yeast is mixed with the dough and left in a warm place. The dough rises and it is then baked.

Pitta bread does not have yeast added to it. It does not rise.

A pot of yeast.

**P**

How could you find out what yeast needs to stay alive?
- What factors might affect how well yeast grows?
- Which factor will you investigate?
- How will you change this factor?
- How will you keep the other factors the same?
- What apparatus will you use?
- What will you look for to see if the yeast is alive in your investigation?
- How will you present your results?
- How will you stay safe?

## How are micro-organisms used to make food?

Bread is made using a fungus called yeast, which makes the bread dough rise.

1 a What is in the dough that yeast feed on?
  b Where have the holes in the baked bread come from?

Bread dough.

Baked bread.

### Cheese

Bacteria are used to make cheese. Milk is first heated to about 70 °C for 16 seconds. This kills most of the bacteria in it, including any dangerous ones. Special bacteria are then added, which feed on the milk and turn it into a lumpy substance, a bit like watery cottage cheese.

The bacteria turn the milk lumpy.

The blue bits in this cheese are types of mould!

The liquid (whey) is removed, leaving only solid bits (curds). The curds are mixed with more bacteria and the cheese is pressed into shape. The cheeses are then left for a time to allow the bacteria to feed on the cheese and give it its flavour. Sometimes a special mould is added to make blue cheese.

The photograph shows some other things that are made using micro-organisms.

2 Why is the milk heated up before cheese making begins?
3 What is whey?
4 Look at the photograph of things made using micro-organisms. Find out how one of them is made.

! On average in the UK, each person eats 9.8 kg of cheese in a year!

**You should know...**

* Micro-organisms help us to make many foods, including bread and cheese.

## What happens when you filter something?

The photograph shows some river water. It is not **pure** water because it has other things in it. It is a **mixture** of water and other things. A *pure* substance has nothing else added to it. For example, pure water only contains water.

1  What is in the jar of river water in the photograph?
2  Explain why water from a river is not pure water.

We can try to get things out of the river water by sieving it. The photograph on the right shows what happens when we do this.

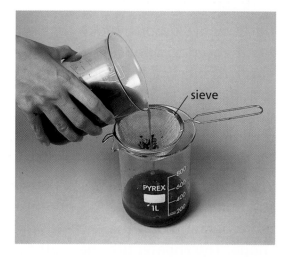

sieve

3  Look at the photograph of sieving.
   a  Is the water that comes through the sieve now pure?
   b  Explain your answer.

When you sieve the river water, the water goes through the holes in the sieve but the stones can't fit through the holes. However, the bits of mud are small enough to fit through the holes and so the water is still not pure.

**Filter paper** has very tiny holes in it. The photograph shows what happens when we put the muddy water through some coffee filter paper. This is called **filtering**.

muddy water

filter paper

4  How do you filter something?

The water that we get from filtering the muddy water *looks* like pure water. However, it is not pure because there are substances **dissolved** in the water. When a substance is dissolved in water, the substance seems to disappear but it is still there. A liquid with something dissolved in it is called a **solution**. Filtering can only take out things that are *not* dissolved.

Here are some liquids.

tap water   sea water   ink   distilled water   orange squash

5 Explain why salty water is not pure water.

- Which of these liquids do you think is pure water?
- How would you find out if you are right? You need to find a way of getting rid of the water to find out if there was anything dissolved in it.

6 The photograph shows a coffee filter. Ground up coffee beans are put into the filter paper and hot water is added. The coffee that you drink collects underneath the filter.

  a Why does the water go brown when it is added to the ground coffee beans?
  b Why don't the ground coffee beans end up in the jug under the filter?

**You should know...**

- What a pure substance is.
- Substances which don't dissolve can be taken out of a liquid by filtering.

## What happens when a solution is evaporated?

The photographs show the first steps in cooking some pasta.

A – Salt is added and stirred.

B – The water boils and some of it *evaporates* and turns into water vapour.

C – Some of the evaporated water has turned back into a liquid on the lid of the pan. The water vapour *condenses* back to water.

1 What happens to the salt in photograph A?
2 What happens to water when it evaporates?
3 a If you were to taste the water that has collected on the lid in photograph C, do you think it will taste salty?
 b Explain your answer.

**P**

Jane is heating blue ink. Some evaporates to become a gas. She makes the gas condense on a tile.

• Will the liquid that collects on the tile be blue?
• Explain why you think this.

When a liquid turns into a gas it is called **evaporation**. Only the liquid can evaporate, so anything dissolved in the liquid will get left behind. If the gas is turned back into a liquid, the liquid will be pure. When a gas turns into a liquid it is called **condensation**.

**You should know...**

• What evaporation and condensation are.
• When a liquid evaporates, anything dissolved in it gets left behind.

**?**

4 Copy this diagram and add the words 'evaporating' and 'condensing' on the arrows, instead of the question marks.

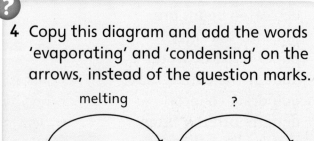
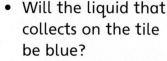
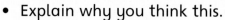

melting          ?

solid        liquid        gas

freezing          ?

## What is distillation?

The car battery in the photograph on the right is being filled with **distilled water**. This is water that has been evaporated and then condensed to make sure that nothing is dissolved in it. It is pure water.

Distilled water is made using apparatus similar to that shown in the diagram below.

In some countries there is not enough water to drink and so they make drinking water from the sea. Large factories, called **desalination plants**, take water out of the sea and heat it up. The steam is condensed and the water is then piped to people's homes for them to drink and wash with.

distilled water

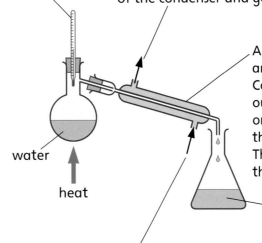

thermometer

water

heat

The tap water comes out of the outer tube of the condenser and goes into the sink.

A condenser has two tubes in it – an inner one and an outer one. Cold water flows through the outer tube to keep the inner one cool. The steam goes down the inner tube and condenses. The liquid water drips out of the inner tube and is collected.

pure water

Cold water, from a tap, goes into the outer tube of the condenser.

*This apparatus can be used for **distillation**.*

*A desalination plant.*

> ?
>
> 1 What is distilled water?
> 2 What happens to water during distillation?
> 3 a Why do you think a condenser has its name?
>   b Why is it important that the inner tube of the condenser is kept cold?
> 4 Find out the name of a country that has desalination plants. Write down where you get your information from.

## How can you dissolve a solid more quickly?

People often add sugar to tea to make it taste sweeter. The sugar dissolves in the tea.

**?**

**1** Write down one other example of something dissolving.

My mum always stirs her tea when she adds sugar. She says that it helps the sugar to dissolve.

I think that the hotter the water is, the faster the sugar will dissolve.

I think that if you have more water, the sugar will dissolve faster.

I don't think the amount of water will make any difference.

My gran always uses spoons of sugar in her tea because she says that sugar lumps take longer to dissolve.

**P**

What you change in an investigation is called a **factor**. Write a list of all the factors that might affect how quickly sugar can dissolve in water.

- Choose one factor to investigate.
- Which factors will you keep the same to make this a **fair test**?
- What apparatus will you use to do your investigation?
- How will you use your apparatus to do the investigation?
- How will you tell when all the sugar has dissolved?
- What will you do to stay safe when you do your investigation?

# 6Cb Graphs and charts

## How can you show your results?

Some children have investigated making things dissolve faster. Their teacher has asked them to draw **line graphs** or **bar charts** of their results.

You use a line graph when there are *numbers* between two measurements that mean something. For example, James used water temperatures of 20 °C, 30 °C and 40 °C but he could have used a temperature between 30 °C and 40 °C (e.g. 35 °C). There are numbers between the temperatures he used which mean something, so he can draw a line graph.

*James needs to decide how to present his results.*

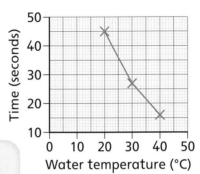

A line graph of James' results. The thing you change always goes on the horizontal axis.

1 Look at the line graph. How long would it take the sugar to dissolve at 35 °C?

In her investigation, Magda changed the brand of sugar she used. There are no numbers between 'Kyle and Sons' and 'Brandon Sugar'! So Magda cannot draw a line graph and she must draw a bar chart.

| Brand of sugar | Time it took for sugar to dissolve (seconds) |
|---|---|
| Pascoe's | 32 |
| Kyle and Sons | 34 |
| Brandon | 29 |

*Magda's results.*

Draw a bar chart or a line graph for each of these tables of results.
- Write down what each set of results shows.
- Write a list of all the ways you can get more sugar to dissolve in water.

| Type of sugar | Time it took for sugar to dissolve (seconds) |
|---|---|
| Caster (fine sugar) | 45 |
| Granulated (coarse sugar) | 27 |
| Icing (powdered sugar) | 16 |

| Water temperature (°C) | Time it took for sugar to dissolve (seconds) |
|---|---|
| 20 | 90 |
| 30 | 60 |
| 40 | 43 |
| 50 | 37 |

| Volume of water (cm³) | Time it took for sugar to dissolve (seconds) |
|---|---|
| 25 | 45 |
| 50 | 47 |
| 75 | 46 |
| 100 | 46 |

## You should know...

- When to draw a bar chart and when to draw a line graph.

# More dissolving

## How much salt will dissolve in water?

Nothing can live in the Dead Sea because it is too salty.

The rocks around the Dead Sea contain a lot of salt, which is dissolved by rain. The salty rain water flows into the Dead Sea where it stays, because there are no rivers out of it.

**?**

1 Why do you think the Dead Sea has this name?

*The Dead Sea is in the Middle East.*

**P**

Jack and Michelle are discussing the Dead Sea.
- Write down a question that could be investigated to find out who is right.
- Plan your investigation.
- How would you make this a fair test?
- How will you know if no more salt is dissolving in your water?
- You should repeat your measurements. Why?

Michelle    Jack

> I think that the Dead Sea must get saltier and saltier because of all the salt that keeps getting into it when it rains.

> I don't think it does keep getting saltier. When I accidentally dropped 20 sugar cubes into my tea, the sugar did not all dissolve and some of it stayed at the bottom. I think the same happens with salt.

The photograph shows all that is left of a sea in Chile. Most of the water has evaporated, leaving the salt behind (the browny white stuff). There is no room in the water that is left to dissolve all the salt and so the salt is all over the ground.

*The remains of a sea in Chile, South America.*

**?**

2 a When the sea in Chile evaporated, why didn't the salt disappear with the water?

b Why didn't the salt stay dissolved in the little lake left by the sea?

3 The bottom of the Dead Sea is covered by salt. Explain why.

### You should know...

- There is a limit to the amount of a substance (such as salt) that can dissolve in water.

## How does the amount of salt in water affect floating?

There are different amounts of salt dissolved in different seas, oceans and rivers.

| Water | Amount of salt (grams of salt per litre of water) |
|---|---|
| Atlantic Ocean | 35 |
| Baltic Sea | 10 |
| Dead Sea | 270 |
| Mediterranean Sea | 38 |
| Red Sea | 41 |
| River water | 0.5 |

*The amount of salt in some different types of water.*

The more salt that is dissolved in the water, the easier it is for things to float. If you go swimming in the Dead Sea you float very easily.

Ships float higher in the water if there is more salt. Ships have Plimsoll lines, to help make sure they do not become too low in the water and sink.

Ships load up with cargo so that the water only comes up to the line for the type of water they are in. Other lines show how much the ship will rise or sink in different types of water.

**?**

3 Look at the table at the top of the page. Which sea would a ship float best in? Explain your answer.
4 If a ship sails from a river into an ocean, will it rise up or sink lower in the water? Explain your answer.

The Plimsoll line was developed by Samuel Plimsoll (1824–1898).

**?**

1 Look at the table. Which sea contains the most salt?
2 Which sea do you think has the most fresh water flowing into it. Explain your answer.

**!** If all the salt in all the seas and oceans were spread over all the land in the world, it would make a layer over 150 metres thick!

*People float very easily in the Dead Sea.*

If the ship is loaded in fresh water and then sails into the sea in winter, the water level will now only come up to this mark.

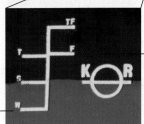

Ships in fresh water should not have water above this line.

*The different letters on the Plimsoll line stand for different types of water.*

## Do all solids dissolve equally well in water?

The photographs show three glasses of sugar solution (sugar dissolved in water).

*Glass A contains 1 spoon of sugar.*  *Glass B contains 3 spoons of sugar.*  *Glass C contains 25 spoons of sugar. No more sugar will dissolve in this water.*

1 How can you tell that no more sugar will dissolve in the water in glass C?

There is a limit to the amount of a solid that can dissolve in water. When we can see that there is some of the solid left, even after stirring for a long time, we know that no more can dissolve.

Some solids dissolve better than others. The table shows how well some solids dissolve in water.

| Substance | How many grams dissolve in 100 cm³ of water |
|---|---|
| aspirin | 0.33 |
| salt | 36 |
| sugar | 204 |
| marble (a rock) | 0 |

2 Look at the table.
  a Which solid dissolves the best?
  b Which solid does not dissolve?
  c How many grams of sugar would dissolve in 200 cm³ of water?

I think all substances will dissolve the same amount.

Gloria

I think that some substances dissolve very well in water and some substances don't dissolve very well.

Harshul

Gloria and Harshul are talking about how different substances dissolve.
Plan an investigation to find out who is right.

sugar   salt   bath salts   instant coffee   stock cubes

• What solids will you compare? You could choose from the ones in the photograph.
• How much water will you use?
• How will you make this a fair test?
• How will you present your results?

### You should know...

• Some substances dissolve easily in water, some dissolve a bit and some do not dissolve at all.

# 6Cd Focus on: Emulsions and foams

## What are emulsions and foams?

### Mixing liquids together

Ethanoic acid is a liquid you may not have heard of, but it is found in vinegar. Vinegar is a **solution** of ethanoic acid in water.

Some salad dressings are made using olive oil and vinegar. You need to shake them up before putting them on your salad because olive oil and vinegar do not mix. The vinegar does not dissolve in the olive oil.

olive oil

vinegar

*Salad dressing.*

*The salad dressing has been shaken up.*

When the salad dressing is shaken up, small droplets of vinegar are mixed into the oil but do not dissolve. When two liquids are mixed like this, it forms an **emulsion**.

### Mixing gases and liquids

Gases will also dissolve in liquids. Most water contains gases from the air that have dissolved in it. Fish breathe the oxygen dissolved in water.

A gas called chlorine is dissolved in tap water by the water companies to kill bacteria that might be in it.

A **liquid foam** is a liquid which has a gas mixed with it, but the gas has not dissolved.

*Shaving foam is a liquid foam.*

**?**

1 What difference can you *see* between an emulsion and a solution?
2 a What is a liquid foam?
  b What do you think a solid foam contains?
3 Say whether each of these is a solution, an emulsion or a liquid foam.

| drinking water | hair styling mousse |
| mayonnaise | milk | vinegar |

4 Which do you think has more dissolved gases in it – hot water or cold water? Explain your reasoning.

33

## What happens when we mix different materials?

Some materials **dissolve** when you put them into water, and some do not.

Mix different materials with water and observe what happens.
- How will you record your results?
- What will you observe if a material dissolves?
- What will you observe if a material does not dissolve?

*The blue powder has dissolved in the water.*

Salt dissolves if you put it into water. You cannot see the salt any more, but you can tell it is still there because the water tastes salty. The dissolved salt and the water make a **solution**. If you let the water in the solution **evaporate**, the salt will be left behind.

**?**

**1 a** What happens to salt if you put it into water?
  **b** How can you get the salt back from the **mixture**?
**2 a** Look at the photograph above. How can you tell that the blue powder has dissolved?
  **b** How could you get the blue powder back from the mixture?

*Flour does not dissolve. If you leave the mixture, the flour will settle on the bottom of the beaker.*

Some materials do not dissolve if you put them in water. A solid that does not dissolve can be separated from the mixture by **filtering**.

**?**

**3 a** How can you tell that flour does not dissolve in water?
  **b** How could you separate the flour from the water?
  **c** Draw a diagram to show how you would do this.

Salt changes when you add it to water, but you can get the salt back again. The change is a **reversible** change. Some changes cannot be changed back again. They are called **irreversible** changes.

Concrete is made by mixing cement with gravel and water. When the concrete dries it forms a new material, which sets and becomes hard. You cannot 'unmix' the concrete to get the cement, gravel and water back. This is an irreversible change.

*Concrete sets to form a very hard material. This change is irreversible.*

Some materials fizz when you put them into water or other liquids. The material changes, and part of it turns into a gas. The gas makes bubbles in the liquid. Changes like this are irreversible.

*Indigestion tablets in water.*

*Vinegar and baking powder.*

## You should know...

- A change is reversible if you can get the original substances back.
- Dissolving is a reversible change.
- A change is irreversible if new materials are made.
- A change is usually irreversible if a gas is made.

**?**

4 a  What does 'reversible' mean?
   b  Describe one change that is reversible.
5  Describe three changes that are irreversible.
6  Plaster can be used to fill holes in walls. You make it by mixing water with a powder.

   a  How will the plaster change when it is put on the wall?
   b  Is this change reversible or irreversible? Explain your answer.

## How much gas is made when you mix different materials?

Baking powder is used to make cakes 'rise'. When baking powder is mixed with water it forms bubbles of gas. The bubbles make foam on top of the water.

**P**

How can you find out how much gas is made when you add baking powder to water?

- Which factors could you change in your investigation?
- Which factor will you change?
- Which factors will you keep the same to make your test fair?
- What will you measure?
- What apparatus will you need?
- How will you present your results?

I think there will be more bubbles if you put more baking powder in.

The bubbles will last longer if I use more baking powder.

I could measure the height of the foam.

Will I need to stir the mixture?

You will get more bubbles if you use more water.

## What happens to materials when you change the temperature?

Heat can make some materials change. If you heat ice, it melts and turns into liquid water. This change is **reversible**, because you can change the liquid water back into a solid again by cooling it down.

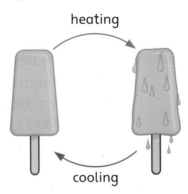

heating

cooling

**?**
1 a What happens to ice if you heat it?
  b How can you reverse this change?
2 a What happens to liquid water if you heat it?
  b Is this change reversible or not? Explain your answer.

Some changes caused by heating are not reversible. Heating changes cake mixture into a cake. You cannot 'uncook' a cake, so this change is **irreversible**.

*Heat can change this...* *...into this.*

clay          unfired clay          fired clay

*Clay has to be 'fired' (heated) to turn it into a hard material.*

**C**
You can make some materials change by heating them. How can you tell if these changes are reversible?
• What observations would you need to make?

You can also change materials by cooling them down, but changes caused by cooling are usually reversible. You can **freeze** water to make ice, but the ice **thaws** and turns back into a liquid again when you let it warm up.

**?**
3 Are these changes reversible or irreversible? Explain your answers.
  a melting chocolate
  b cooking an egg
  c freezing peas
  d cooling down steam
  e heating clay

### You should know...
• Heating and cooling some materials can cause them to change.
• Some changes caused by heating are irreversible.
• Changes caused by cooling are usually reversible.

# What new materials can be made by heating limestone?

**Limestone** is a type of rock found in many parts of the country. It is very useful as a building material, but other useful materials can be made by heating it.

*Limestone is useful as a building material.*

Heating limestone changes it into a new material called **lime**, or **quicklime**. Lime can be spread on fields to make it easier for some kinds of plant to grow in the soil. It can also be used to make cement.

Quicklime has been made in **lime kilns** since Roman times. This lime kiln was built 2000 years ago and is still in use today.

Quicklime can be changed into another new material by adding water to it. This new material is called **slaked lime**. Slaked lime can be used as **limewash** on the outside of houses. As it dries it absorbs a gas called **carbon dioxide** from the air, and this turns it into a hard, weatherproof coating.

*Lime can be spread on fields to improve the soil.*

*This house has been painted with limewash.*

**?**

1 Describe one use for each of the following:
   a limestone
   b quicklime
   c slaked lime.

2 a How is limestone changed to quicklime?
   b How is quicklime changed to slaked lime?
   c What happens to limewash as it dries?

3 Copy and complete this flow chart to show how limestone can be changed.

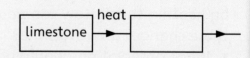

## What happens when materials burn?

Some materials change when you heat them. If you make a material hot enough, it may burn. You can usually see a flame when something is burning, and you can feel that the burning material is giving off heat. Burning is an irreversible change, because new materials are formed.

1 Name two materials that are burnt to give heat.
2 What is left after wood has burnt?

*Natural gas* burns with a blue flame. It produces invisible gases when it burns. The heat it gives off is used to cook food or to keep homes warm.

Log fires can be used to heat houses. **Ash** is left after the wood has burnt, and gases are given off. This is an irreversible change.

The wax burns.

melted wax

Candles are made of wax. When you light a candle, heat from the match makes some of the wax melt and evaporate to form a gas. This is a reversible change. The wax gas burns and forms new materials – this is an irreversible change.

Which materials burn the easiest?
• Which materials could you test?
• How easy is it to set them alight?
• What is left after they have burnt?

3 Which part of a candle burns?
4 How can you tell that burning is an irreversible change?

**You should know...**
• Burning is an irreversible change.
• New materials are made when materials burn.

# 6Dc Fire safety

## How can we keep ourselves safe from fire?

Burning materials produce a lot of heat. Fires can cause burns, which are very painful, and very bad burns can kill you. Some of the new materials made by burning can be harmful. If a house catches fire, people can die from breathing in the smoke and gases.

*Some furniture gives off poisonous gases when it burns.*

*Smoke alarms can detect a fire and warn people to get out of the house.*

! The fire brigade is called out to over 70 000 fires in homes every year. Nearly 500 people die in these fires, and over 14 000 people are injured. Many of the injuries and deaths happen when people breathe in the smoke.

You can help to prevent fires by:
- never leaving clothes or toys near to fires or heaters
- never playing with matches or fire
- unplugging electrical things when you have finished using them.

? 
1 Describe two ways that a fire in your home could harm you.
2 Make a poster to tell younger children how to prevent fires at home.

### You should know...
- Some of the new materials made in burning are harmful.
- How to prevent fires.

## How are forest fires put out?

Fires in forests can destroy a lot of trees. Fires can threaten people's lives or homes if they happen close to villages or towns. Forest fires usually happen in the summer when the wood is dry.

In countries like Russia, Canada and the USA there are very large areas of forest. Fires can happen a long way from roads, so it is sometimes very difficult to get to the fire to try to control it or to put it out. It is easier to put out a fire when it is still small, so helicopters are sometimes used to drop water on the fires, or to take fire fighters to the fire. However, aeroplanes can fly faster than helicopters, so fire fighters sometimes parachute out of an aeroplane to a place near the fire. The men and women who do this are called **smokejumpers**.

Smokejumpers try to stop fires spreading. They can do this by cutting down trees in the path of the fire. When the fire comes to the gap it will go out because there is no more wood to burn.

Smokejumpers often have to parachute into a forest or are dropped from a helicopter on a long rope.

**?**

1 Which countries use smokejumpers to put out fires?
2 a Why do smokejumpers travel to fires in aeroplanes?
  b Why do they need to use parachutes?
3 a How do smokejumpers try to stop fires spreading?
  b Why does this work?
4 Find out what equipment smokejumpers take with them, and what they use it for.

Smokejumping can be a dangerous job!

## What can forces do?

**Forces** are pushes or pulls, and they are all around us. We cannot see forces, but we can see what they do.

If you pull on a spring, you can feel it pulling back.

**?**

1 What can you feel if you try to pull on a spring?

The force from a magnet lets you pick up things like paper clips.

*Magnets.*

*Springy toys.*

**?**

2 What material are the paper clips made from? Explain your answer.

**?**

3 a What causes the friction that slows down the parachute?
  b How could you make this friction bigger?
4 Why is there not much friction between the ice and the children's shoes?
5 Think about riding downhill on a bicycle. Make a list of all the different forces and describe what they do.

**Friction** is a force that slows down moving things. Friction can happen between solid surfaces, or it can be caused by air or water.

*A toy parachute.*

*The ice is very smooth, so there is not much friction between the ice and the children's shoes.*

### You should know...

- Forces are pushes or pulls.
- There are different kinds of force.

## What is weight and how can we measure it?

You can measure forces using a **forcemeter**. The forcemeter in the photograph is being used to measure the force of friction between the wood and the table. The units for measuring force are **newtons (N)**.

This forcemeter is being used to find the **weight** of the grapes. When we weigh something, the weight of the object stretches the spring inside the forcemeter and moves the pointer. Weight is a force, and so we measure weight in newtons.

⏳ The units for force are named after Sir Isaac Newton (1642–1727), who studied forces and gravity.

❓
1 What can we use to measure a force?
2 What is the unit for measuring forces?
3 a What is the weight of the grapes doing to the forcemeter?
 b What will happen if there are two bunches of grapes on the forcemeter?

A force called **gravity** pulls objects towards the Earth. The weight of an object is caused by the Earth's gravity pulling on it. The object also pulls the Earth towards it.

The Moon also attracts objects towards it. The force of gravity is less on the Moon than it is on the Earth, so things do not weigh as much.

Astronauts on the Moon.

The box is pulled towards the Earth.

The Earth is pulled towards the box.

❓
4 Why do astronauts walk differently on the Moon than they do on the Earth?

### You should know...

- How to measure forces.
- The units for force are newtons (N).
- Weight is a force caused by gravity.

# What are balanced forces, and what do they do?

*The forces on the book are balanced, so it is not moving.*

If you hold a book in your hand, you can feel gravity pulling down on the book. The weight of the book is pulling downwards, so you have to give an upwards force from your hand to stop the book falling. The force from your hand is the same size as the weight of the book, but the two forces are in opposite directions. The forces are **balanced**, so the book is not moving.

We can use arrows to show forces. The arrow points in the same direction as the force, and the size of the arrow shows you how big the force is.

1 Look at the photograph of the book.
   a What is the downwards force on the book?
   b Why isn't the book moving?

All **stationary** (still) objects have balanced forces on them.

*This man is climbing a big cliff. It will take him two days, so he is going to sleep on this 'portaledge'.*

*This woman is studying plants in the rainforest. She is using a rope to help her to get to the tops of the trees.*

2 Look at the photograph above.
   a Where is the upwards force coming from?
   b How big is the upwards force compared to the downwards force?
   c Explain your answer to part b.

3 Sketch a picture of the woman, and draw arrows on the picture to show the forces.

Balanced forces can be horizontal as well as vertical. The dog is trying to reach the bone, but the force from the lead is stopping it from moving. The two forces are the same size and in opposite directions, so they are balanced.

Robert Hooke (1635–1703) was a scientist who lived at the same time as Sir Isaac Newton. Hooke studied how materials behave when they are stretched, and this work led to the invention of the forcemeter.

We use ideas about balanced forces when we weigh things. The scales that are being used to weigh the baby in the photograph below have a spring inside them. The spring stretches until its pulling force balances the weight of the baby.

**?**

4 Explain why the dog in the picture is not moving.
5 Describe the forces on the baby in the photograph.

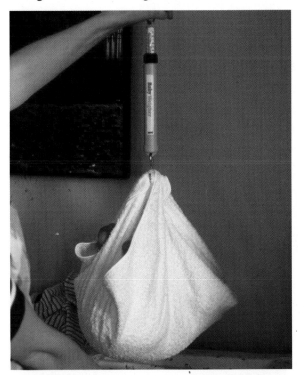

**C**

You can measure the length of an elastic band with weights hanging from it to find out how it stretches.

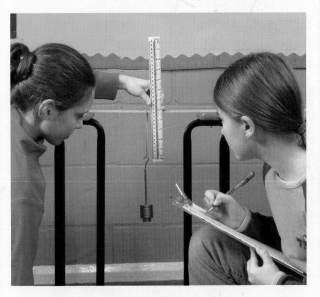

### You should know...

- Stationary objects have balanced forces on them.
- We can use arrows to show the direction and size of forces.

- How can you present your measurements to help you to find patterns in your results?

## Why do some things float?

If you have ever tried to pick up something heavy under water, you will know that it feels much heavier when you get it out of the water.

*Some things do not feel very heavy when they are under water.*

*They feel much heavier when you lift them out of the water.*

**0**

You can use a forcemeter to find out how water affects the weight of an object.

• Why should you weigh your objects more than once?

When an object is in water, the water pushes up on it. The upwards force from the water is called **upthrust**. The upthrust cancels out some of the downwards pull of gravity, so the object does not seem to weigh as much.

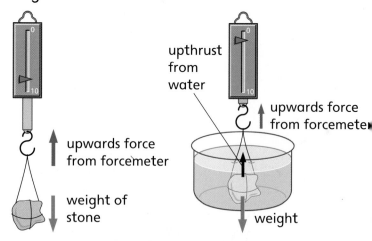

upthrust from water

upwards force from forcemeter

upwards force from forcemeter

weight of stone

weight

*The upwards force from the forcemeter balances the weight of the stone.*

*The upthrust from the water balances part of the weight of the stone, so the force from the forcemeter does not need to be as big. Both the upwards forces are balancing the weight of the stone.*

? 
1 What is the upwards force from water called?
2 Why is it easier to pick up a stone if it is under water?
3 If the weight of the stone was 2 N, and the upthrust was 1 N, what weight would the forcemeter show?

Sometimes there is enough upthrust from the water to completely balance the weight of the object. When the upthrust is equal to the weight, the object floats.

*You float when the upthrust balances your weight.*

upthrust from the water balances the weight

weight

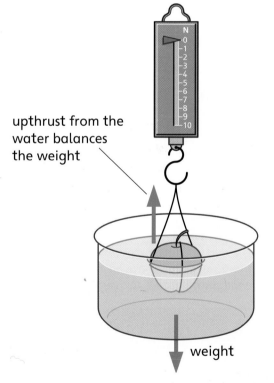

*The apple is floating, so the upthrust is completely balancing the weight. The forcemeter is reading zero.*

? 
4 If your weight is 300 N, what is the upthrust on you when you are floating in water?
5 The upthrust on a boat is 1000 N. What is the weight of the boat?

! Ice floats on water. This means that when ponds freeze in the winter, the ice forms on top of the water and the water underneath it stays liquid. If this did not happen the pond would freeze from the bottom upwards and all the animals living in it would die.

## You should know...

- There is an upwards force when an object is in water, called upthrust.
- When something floats, the upthrust balances the weight.

## What can unbalanced forces do?

This car has started to move because the force from its engine is bigger than the force of friction.

This car has stopped because the friction force in the brakes is bigger than the force from the engine.

Stationary objects have balanced forces on them. When the forces on something are **unbalanced**, an object can

- start or stop moving
- speed up or slow down
- change the direction it is moving.

The cup will fall faster and faster until it hits the floor, because the air resistance is not enough to balance its weight.

You speed up near the top of a slide, because the friction is not enough to balance the downwards force.

Friction slows you down at the bottom of the slide, because now there is no force pulling you forwards.

**?**

1 a Make a list of five things that unbalanced forces can do to an object.
  b Describe one example for each of the things on your list.

The force from the bat makes the ball change direction.

### You should know...

- What unbalanced forces can do to an object.

## How long do spinners take to fall?

**Air resistance** is a force that slows down moving objects. If a falling object has a lot of air resistance, it will fall more slowly.

Sycamore seeds spin when they fall, so they fall more slowly. You can make a spinner out of paper, like this.

Which factors could you change in this investigation?

- Which factor will you investigate?
- How will you make your test fair?
- What apparatus will you need?
- How many times will you repeat each measurement?
- How will you present your results?

I think the size of the wings will make a difference.

Putting more paper clips on will make it fall faster.

It will take longer to fall if you drop it from higher up.

It will work better if you make it from card instead of paper.

I think the wings need to be twisted to make it spin properly.

# 6Ed  Air resistance

## What can air resistance do?

**Air resistance** is a force that slows down moving objects. This parachutist has jumped out of an aeroplane, but he can land safely because the parachute provides a lot of air resistance. The air resistance acts in the opposite direction to his weight.

Air resistance can also be used to slow objects moving along the ground. This drag racing car is moving very fast when it crosses the finish line. It uses a parachute to help it to slow down.

air resistance

weight

1 Why do parachutes need to be large?
2 Sketch the drag racer. Draw an arrow on your picture to show the direction of the air resistance force.

The time an object takes to fall depends on its air resistance. Everything would fall at the same speed if there was no air resistance. Astronaut Dave Scott demonstrated this when he went to the Moon. He dropped a hammer and a feather, and they both landed at the same time. This happens because there is no air on the Moon, so there is no force of air resistance on moving objects.

3 a Which two forces will affect a feather if you drop it?
  b Sketch a feather, and add labelled arrows to show these two forces.
  c Draw another picture of a feather, and show the forces that would act on it if you dropped it on the Moon.
4 Explain why a hammer falls faster than a feather if you drop them on Earth.

### You should know...

- Air resistance is a force that slows down moving objects.
- Air resistance on a falling object acts in the opposite direction to the weight.

# Focus on: Air resistance in nature

## How do plants and animals use air resistance?

Plants reproduce by making seeds. The seeds need to move away from the parent plant, so that they are not competing with it for water or light. Some seeds rely on the wind to move them.

*Willowherb seeds are light and fluffy. The wind can blow them a long way.*

*Seeds of the lime tree spin as they fall.*

**?**

1 **a** What feature of willowherb seeds gives them a large air resistance?
  **b** Why is this an advantage to the plant?
2 **a** How does spinning affect the air resistance of lime seeds?
  **b** Name one other tree whose seeds spin as they fall.

Some baby animals need to move away from their parents. Spiderlings (baby spiders) need to move away from their hatching place before they build their own webs, so there is enough food for them all. Some spiders move away by making a long silk thread. The wind catches the thread, and blows the spider away. This is called 'ballooning'.

Other animals use air resistance to help them to move around.

*Baby spiders ballooning.*

*Flying squirrels do not really fly. They use flaps of skin between their front and back legs to increase their air resistance. This helps them to glide between branches when they are moving through trees.*

**?**

3 **a** Why do baby spiders need to move away from where they hatched?
  **b** How do some spiders do this?
4 How do flying squirrels use air resistance?
5 Find out how flying lizards increase their air resistance.

## How do we see lights? Why do we get shadows?

We need light to see things.

*If there is no light, we cannot see anything!*

The torch is making light. It is a **light source**. The light is travelling from the torch to the cat. The light can travel through the air, because the air is **transparent**.

There is a **shadow** behind the cat, because the light cannot go through the cat. The cat is **opaque**.

Light travels in straight lines. We can show the direction light is travelling by drawing a straight line with an arrow on it.

**?**

**1**

**a** What is making the light in this photograph?

**b** Why is there a shadow behind the singer?

**2** Write a list of five light sources.

We can see the Sun, and other things that make light, because the light goes into our eyes.

John can see the television, because light from the television can reach his eyes.

Sally cannot see the Sun. Her hat stops the light from the Sun getting to her eyes.

**?**

3 Why does a sunhat keep sunlight out of your eyes?
4 Sunil is shining a torch at the wall. Draw a diagram to show how he can make a shadow of his hand on the wall.
5 You are looking at a candle. Draw a diagram to show how you can see the candle flame.

Some materials are **translucent**. Light can go through them, but you cannot see things clearly through them. Bathroom windows are often made of translucent glass.

*This window is made out of translucent glass.*

## You should know...

- Light travels in straight lines from a light source.
- Materials can be transparent, translucent or opaque.
- A shadow is formed when an opaque material blocks light.
- You can see lights because light goes into your eyes.

## How do we see things in mirrors?

We use **mirrors** for lots of things.

A beam of light changes direction when it hits a mirror. The thing we see in a mirror is called the **image**. We see images because mirrors **reflect** light, and the light goes into our eyes.

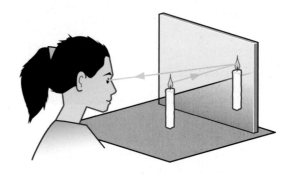

**?**

**1 a** Write down three people who might use a mirror.
  **b** Why do these people need to use mirrors?

We can show what is happening to the light by drawing straight lines with arrows on them.

**?**

**2** What is the light source in the cartoon?
**3** What does the mirror do?

### You should know...

• Mirrors reflect light.
• Light changes direction when it is reflected.
• We see things in mirrors because the reflected light goes into our eyes.

## When were mirrors invented?

Small hand mirrors have been used for thousands of years. The ancient Greeks and Romans used mirrors made out of smooth, polished metal – usually bronze, tin or silver. Polishing the metal made it very shiny. Mirrors big enough to look at the whole body were not made until about 2000 years ago.

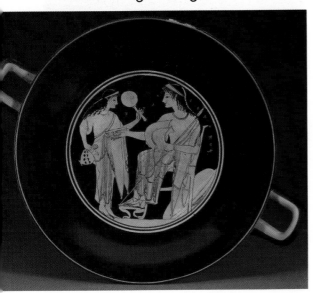

Modern mirrors are usually made of glass coated with a very thin layer of aluminium or silver metal on the back. The first mirrors made of glass with a metal backing were made in about 1200, and the metal used was a mixture of tin and mercury. Those mirrors did not have an aluminium backing, because aluminium metal could not be manufactured until 1859. The first glass mirrors were very expensive, so only rich people had them.

The best mirrors are the ones with the smoothest reflecting surfaces. In glass mirrors, it is actually the metal coating that reflects the light. Glass mirrors reflect light better than metal ones because the metal is very smooth where it is stuck to the glass.

**?**

1 What were the first mirrors made from?
2 What are modern mirrors made from?
3 Which part of a modern mirror actually reflects the light?
4 Why do modern mirrors reflect light better than the first mirrors?
5 Why didn't the first glass mirrors have aluminium coatings?
6 Write down a list of all the different metals mentioned in the passage.
7 How can you see your reflection without a mirror?

**!** Today, mirrors are used in telescopes that are used to look at the stars. The biggest mirrors can be over 8 metres across!

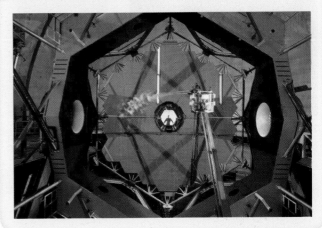

# 6Fc Shiny or dull?

## Which materials reflect light best?

Some materials reflect light very well. Some materials hardly reflect any light at all.

These clothes are good at reflecting light. The material has lots of small, shiny pieces of metal on it.

Shiny surfaces reflect light better than dull ones. Shiny surfaces are usually very smooth.

1 Why do the clothes in the picture reflect a lot of light?

How could you investigate which materials are best at reflecting light?
- Which materials will you test?
- How will you test them?
- How can you make sure your test is fair?

You can make a piece of wood shiny by polishing it. Polishing makes the surface smoother.

2 Why does polishing something make it shiny?

3

The surface of the wood is rough before it is polished.

The surface is smoother after it has been polished.

a Why can't you see your reflection in this car?
b What could you do to the car so that you could see your reflection?

### You should know...

- Shiny surfaces reflect light better than dull surfaces.

56

## How can your clothes help to keep you safe?

People who work near traffic often wear special clothing so that drivers can see them easily. This safety clothing is usually bright yellow, with special strips of reflective material.

Everyone has to use the roads at some time. If you are walking along a road in the dark, drivers will be able to see you more easily if you are wearing reflective clothing. If you haven't got special clothing, wearing light-coloured clothes will be safer than wearing dark ones. When you are riding a bicycle, you must make sure that it has lights on it.

*Safety clothing is often yellow so that drivers can see it easily.*

*These children are going for a cycle ride.*

*This is what they look like when it is getting dark.*

**?**

1 Why do people working near roads need to wear special clothing?

2 Why should you wear light-coloured clothing at night?

3 Look at the pictures of the children with bicycles.

  a Whose clothes are better for cycling at night? Explain why.

  b Which bicycle is safer for cycling at night? Explain why.

## How can you change a shadow?

**?** How can you find out what affects the size of a shadow?
- What factors might make a difference?
- Which one will you investigate?
- How will you make your investigation fair?
- What equipment will you need?

I think the shadow will move if you move the torch.

If you move the torch nearer the screen the shadow will get smaller.

I don't think it matters where the torch is.

The shadow will get bigger if you move the card nearer to the screen.

You can only make a bigger shadow if the card is bigger.

## What is an eclipse?

The Moon goes around the Earth once every 28 days. Sometimes the Moon gets between the Sun and the Earth and this causes a **solar eclipse**. This means that part of the Earth is in the shadow of the Moon.

If you are standing in the shadow of the Moon, you will see the Sun being blocked out. If all the Sun is blocked out, it is known as a **total eclipse**. If only part of the Sun is blocked out, it is called a **partial eclipse**.

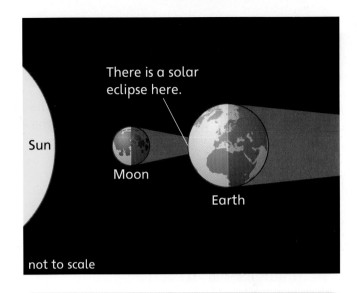

There is a solar eclipse here.

Sun

Moon

Earth

not to scale

The Moon is not a light source. We can see the Moon because it reflects light from the Sun. Sometimes the Moon goes into the shadow of the Earth. When this happens we cannot see the Moon properly. This is a **lunar eclipse**.

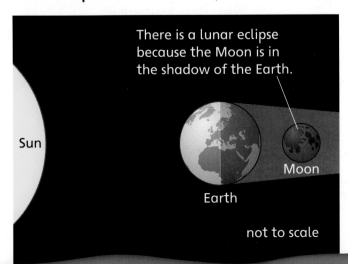

There is a lunar eclipse because the Moon is in the shadow of the Earth.

Sun

Earth

Moon

not to scale

! The last total solar eclipse visible in the UK happened on 11 August 1999. The total eclipse could only be seen from Cornwall. A quarter of a million people travelled to Cornwall to see it.

? 
1 What is a solar eclipse?
2 Describe what you might see and feel if you watched a solar eclipse.
3 Why can you only see a solar eclipse from small parts of the Earth? (*Hint*: Look carefully at the diagram.)
4 What is the difference between a solar eclipse and a lunar eclipse?

## How do electrical circuits work?

Many things around us use electricity. Electrical **components** such as bulbs and motors only work when they are in a complete **circuit**.

> **?**
>
> 1 Which part of the circuit provides the electricity?
> 2 a Why is the inside of a wire made of metal?
>   b Why is the outside of a wire made of plastic?
>   c How does the plastic help to keep you safe?

The **battery** provides the electricity.

The inside of the wire is made of metal because metal is an **electrical conductor**. Electricity can flow through metals easily.

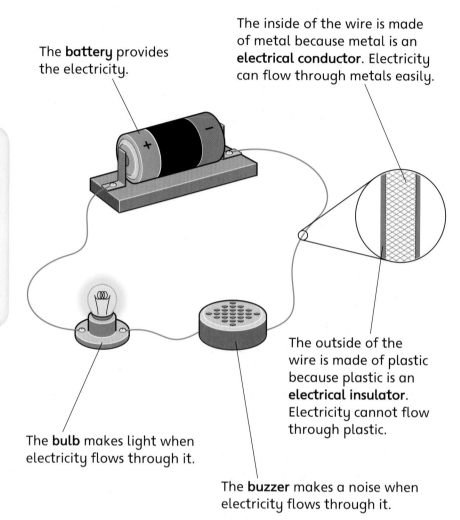

The outside of the wire is made of plastic because plastic is an **electrical insulator**. Electricity cannot flow through plastic.

The **bulb** makes light when electricity flows through it.

The **buzzer** makes a noise when electricity flows through it.

This toy windmill has a **motor** to make the sails go around, and a **switch** to turn it on and off.

> **?**
>
> 3 Look at the circuit for the toy windmill.
>   a How could you make the sails move around?
>   b Explain why this will work.

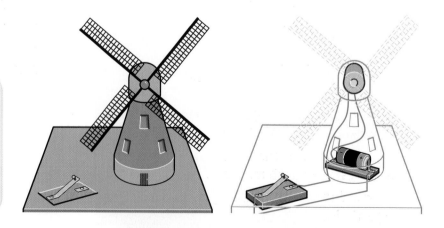

Matt has made a sign with his name on.
It lights up when he presses the switch.
Pressing the switch completes the circuit.

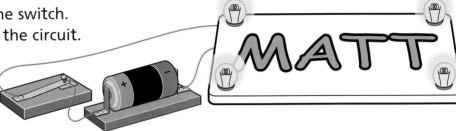

The bulb in this table lamp is much brighter than the bulbs in Matt's sign. The table lamp uses **mains electricity**.

**?**

4 Why shouldn't Matt use bulbs like the one in the table lamp?
5 Matt wants to make the bulbs in his sign brighter. How could he do this?
6 Matt changes his circuit so that he only has two bulbs. What will happen to the brightness of the bulbs?

It is important to match the components in the circuit to each other. If the battery does not have a big enough **voltage**, bulbs will not light and motors will not turn. If the battery provides too much voltage the bulb may break.

*This bulb is broken because too much electricity flowed through it.*

**?**

7 One of the bulbs in this circuit is broken. Why won't the other bulb light?

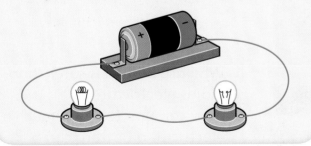

Alessandro Volta (1745–1827) made the first electric battery in 1800. It was made of lots of discs of metal.

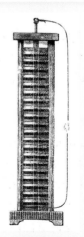

## You should know...

• Metals are electrical conductors and plastics are electrical insulators.
• What different components in a circuit do.
• How to change the brightness of bulbs in a circuit.

## How can we use electricity safely?

Personal stereos, electronic games and torches all use batteries to provide electricity. Batteries are safe to use because they do not provide much electricity. The voltage number written on the side of a battery tells you how much electricity it can supply. For instance, a 3 volt (3 V) battery provides twice as much electricity as a 1.5 V battery.

Bigger machines like fridges, cookers and washing machines need more power, so they use mains electricity. Mains electricity that comes into houses and schools has a voltage of 230 V. The voltage in overhead electricity wires is even higher. An **electric shock** from mains electricity could hurt you or even kill you. However, mains electricity is safe as long as you follow some simple rules.

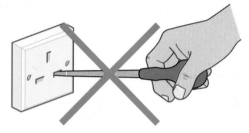

- Never touch the bare metal parts of plugs, or poke things into sockets.
- Never open up electrical equipment. You can sometimes get an electric shock even if it is not still plugged in.
- Don't use anything electrical near water.

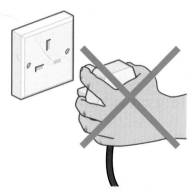

- Never play near places with warning signs like this.

- Do not fly kites or use fishing rods near electricity wires.

**?**
1 Why are batteries safer than mains electricity?
2 How can you tell how much electricity a battery can supply?
3 Design a poster for children in Year 1 to warn them about the dangers of mains electricity.

## How can rechargeable batteries be used?

Small batteries like the ones in radios or torches make electricity from the chemicals inside them. When all the chemicals are used up the battery stops working.

Some batteries can be **recharged** by passing electricity through them. Cars need batteries to start the engine, and to make the headlights work. It takes a lot of electricity to start an engine, so car batteries are much bigger than the batteries in torches. When the car is moving, part of the engine called an **alternator** makes electricity to recharge the battery.

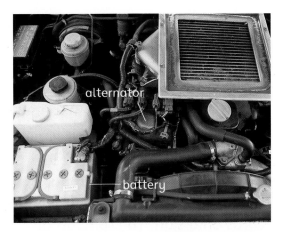

alternator

battery

This buoy warns ships about a rock under the water. The light on the top is lit at night, and uses electricity from a battery inside the buoy. The **solar cells** on the buoy make electricity when the sun shines on them, and this electricity is used to recharge the battery.

The yacht below uses a battery for starting the engine, and to make the lights and radio work. The battery can be recharged when the yacht is using its engine, and the **wind turbine** on the back can also make electricity to recharge the battery.

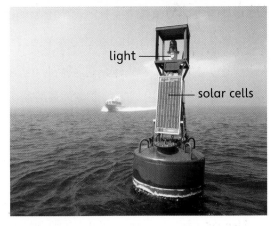

light

solar cells

wind turbine

**?**

1 Why do cars need batteries?
2 Why do buoys need to be lit up at night?
3 Name three different ways of making electricity to recharge batteries.
4 If a driver leaves the car headlights on when the car is parked, the battery will eventually run out of electricity. Why doesn't this happen when the car is on a long journey at night?
5 Fire engines need much larger batteries than cars, and they get recharged from the mains when the fire engine is in its garage.
  a Why do fire engines need large batteries?
  b Why do they need to be recharged from the mains?

# 6Gb Drawing circuits

## How can we draw electrical circuits?

A **symbol** is a shape that represents something else. Symbols make things easier and quicker to write down and to understand.

In mathematics you use symbols for numbers and to tell you what to do with them. It is much quicker to write 36 + 54 = 90 than it is to write 'if you add fifty four to thirty six you get ninety'.

Symbols are used on the roads as well. A driver can see what the symbol means more easily than she could read words on a sign. The symbols also make it easier for people from other countries to understand the signs.

We can use symbols to draw electrical circuits.

It is much easier to draw this:   than this:

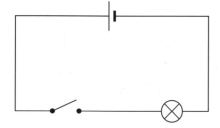

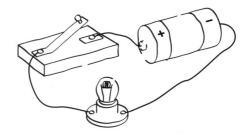

*This is a **circuit diagram**.*

If you have a really complicated circuit, like this one inside a TV, you couldn't draw it unless you used symbols. Engineers need to use circuit diagrams when they repair broken televisions or computers, because they need to understand how the circuits work.

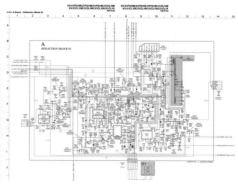

**?**

1  Why do we use symbols in maths and for road signs?

**?**

2  Why do engineers use symbols to show electrical circuits?

We always use the same symbol for each component, so that anyone who looks at a circuit diagram can understand it.

| Component | | Symbol |
|---|---|---|
| | one cell | —│├— |
| | two cells (a battery) | —┤├┤├— |
| | wire | —— |
| | open switch | —o⟋o— |
| | closed switch | —o—o— |
| | bulb | —⊗— |
| | buzzer | ⊻ |
| | motor | —Ⓜ— |

Most people call this a battery, but its proper scientific name is a **cell**.

A battery is two or more cells used together, like this:

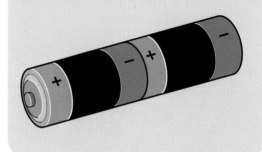

❓

3 Draw neat copies of the symbols for a cell, a bulb and an open switch.

4 Draw a circuit diagram for this circuit.

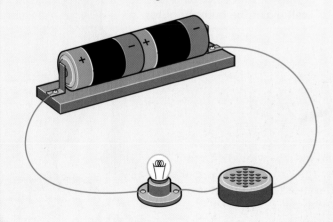

5 Draw a picture to show what this circuit looks like. Label the components on your drawing.

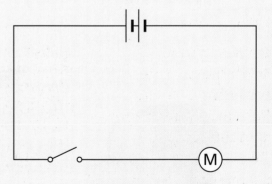

## You should know...

- Why we use symbols to draw electrical circuits.
- The symbols for different components.

## How can wires change the brightness of bulbs?

You can change the brightness of bulbs in a circuit by changing the number of cells or the number of bulbs.

**P**

How can you find out what happens when you put a piece of thin wire into the circuit?

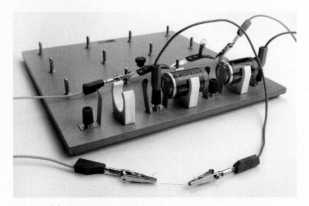

- Which factors could you change?
- Which factor will you investigate?
- What apparatus will you need?

I think a longer piece of wire will make the bulbs dimmer.

I think a thin piece of wire will make the bulbs brighter.

Does it matter what kind of metal the wire is made of?

We could put the wire in different places in the circuit. Will this make any difference to the brightness?

# Changing circuits

## Why does changing the circuit change the brightness?

You can make bulbs brighter by adding more cells to a circuit. If there are more cells, there is more electricity flowing around the circuit, so the bulbs are brighter.

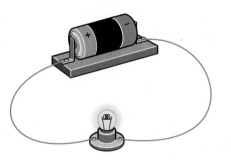
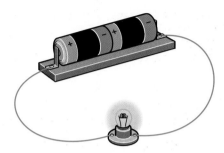

You can make bulbs dimmer by adding more of them to a circuit. It is difficult for electricity to flow through bulbs. If you add more bulbs, it is more difficult for electricity to flow through them all, and so less electricity flows through the circuit. Bulbs are dimmer when there is less electricity flowing.

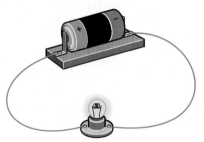
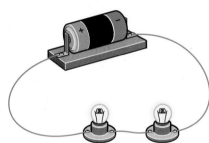

You can also make bulbs dimmer by putting a piece of thin wire in the circuit. It is harder for electricity to flow through thin wire than thick wire, so less electricity flows and the bulbs are dimmer. It is also harder for electricity to flow through long wires, so a long piece of wire will give dimmer bulbs than a short piece of wire.

**?**

1 a Write down one way of making bulbs in a circuit brighter.
  b Explain why this works.
2 a Write down one way of making bulbs in a circuit dimmer.
  b Explain why this works.
3 You can make bulbs brighter by using fewer of them in a circuit. Explain why this works.

**?**

4 a Which piece of wire is it easiest for electricity to flow through?
    A long and thick
    B short and thick
    C long and thin
  b Explain your answer to part a.

### You should know...

• How the length and thickness of a piece of wire can affect the amount of electricity flowing in a circuit.

The Smith family are spending the day in the water park at Adventureworld.

The water park is made out of different **materials** that have different **properties**. The slide is held up by **metal** bars that are **strong** and **rigid** (stiff). The slide is made of thick plastic because it is **hard** and won't wear away. The ring that Emma is using is made of rubber because it is **flexible** and so it is comfortable to sit on.

**?**

1  Why do the bars that hold up the slides need to be strong and rigid?
2  **a**  Why is the front of the cabinet in the food stall made of glass? Use the word **transparent** in your answer.
   **b**  What does the word **opaque** mean?
3  There are some notes stuck to the fridge in the kiosk using **magnets**. Write down the name of one magnetic material.
4  How hot is the water in the shallow pool?
5  What properties of a towel make it useful for drying ourselves with?

The pool water is **sieved** and **filtered** to take out things that don't **dissolve** (**insoluble** things), like hair, dead leaves and sand. Large things, for example dead leaves, are collected by a sieve. Smaller things, such as hair and sand, will go through the sieve but are removed by a **filter**.

*A swimming pool sieve.*

**?**

6 From the picture on the opposite page, name one **solid** that is:
   a soluble        b insoluble.
7 How can you separate a mixture of sand and water?

**?**

8 The first two stages in the **water cycle** are water evaporating and then condensing to form clouds. What are the next stages in the water cycle?

Extra water is added to the pools in Adventureworld because a lot of water **evaporates** during the day. When water evaporates, it forms a **gas** called **water vapour**. If water vapour cools down again, it will **condense** (turn back into a **liquid**). This is how clouds form.

The water in Grandpa's coffee is also evaporating. The warmer a liquid is, the faster it will evaporate. If the liquid is **boiling**, it is evaporating as fast as it can. When a liquid evaporates, things that are dissolved in it are left behind.

The coffee is in a plastic foam cup to keep it warm. This type of plastic is a good heat **insulator**, which means that it does not let heat go through it.

*A plastic foam drinks cup.*

**?**

9 Grandpa's coffee is a **mixture** of water, sugar and 'coffee solids' (it is a **solution**). What would be left behind if all of the water in Grandpa's coffee evaporated?
10 Stuart did an investigation using a cup of coffee like Grandpa's. The graph shows the results.
   a What question do you think was being investigated?
   b What would the line of the graph be like if the investigation was done on a colder day?
11 a How were the ice cubes in Grandma's drink made?
   b What is happening to the ice cubes?

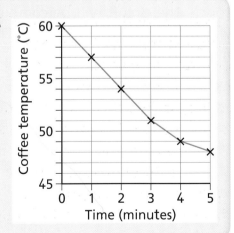

Side stalls

The Smith family are looking at some stalls at Adventureworld. All the things around them are made out of **solids**, **liquids** or **gases** (the three **states of matter**). Solids keep their shapes and their **volumes**. Liquids can flow and take up the shapes of the containers they are in, but keep their volumes. Gases flow all over the place, fill the containers they are in and don't keep their volumes (they can be squashed).

James is trying to win a goldfish. If the **metal** hoop touches the metal wire he will not win! The wire and the hoop are part of an electrical **circuit**. If they touch, the circuit will be completed and **electricity** will flow, making a bell ring. This works because metals **conduct** electricity.

1 From the picture above, write down the names of:
   a a solid
   b a liquid
   c a gas.
2 What are these gases used for?
   a helium
   b carbon dioxide
3 What **evidence** is there in the picture that liquids change shape?

metal, e.g. **copper** or steel

4 What is ...
   a an **electrical conductor**
   b an **electrical insulator**?
5 a What type of metal is used inside the wires around our homes?
   b Why are electrical plugs made out of plastic?

The rocks in the waterfall have different properties. You can see some of these properties (such as what they look like) but you need to do tests to find out about other properties. Rocks like marble, slate and granite are hard and don't let water through them (they are **impermeable** ). Rocks like chalk and limestone are not so hard. They are **permeable** to water because they have tiny holes in them.

**?**

6 Look at the pictures of the rocks below. Which of the rocks will wear away the quickest when they are put under a waterfall. Explain your answer.

Some rocks, like limestone, can be changed permanently if vinegar is added to them. The rock changes into different substances. This is an example of an **irreversible change**. Irreversible changes also happen when things burn.

*Adding vinegar to crushed limestone.*

**?**

7 What evidence is there in the photograph on the left that adding vinegar to limestone is an irreversible change?
8 Look at the picture at the top of page 70. Find an example of something that has been made by an irreversible change.

"Look, I'm getting taller!"

A
Grandpa
D
Grandma
Dad
James
C
Stuart
Mum
B
Emma

The Smith family have stopped to have some lunch at Adventureworld. Some members of the family are eating **balanced** meals and others are not.

**?**

1 Write down three reasons why you need food.
2 a Name two different sorts of carbohydrates.
  b Why are carbohydrates needed in your diet?
3 Is Dad eating a balanced meal? Explain your answer.
4 Humans and other animals all **feed, move, grow** and **reproduce**. These are called **life processes**. The boxes (A–D) in the picture show some life processes. Which life process does each box show?
5 These are the stages in a human life: **adult, teenage** (or **adolescence**), **babyhood, old age, childhood**.
  a Write this list out in order, from youngest to oldest.
  b Which stage are each of the people in the picture above in?

Foods containing **vitamins, minerals** and **fibre** are important for health.

Foods containing a **carbohydrate** called **starch** are important for energy.

Foods containing **proteins** are important for growth.

Foods containing **fat** are important for energy.

Foods containing a **carbohydrate** called **sugar** are used for energy. Too much sugar may cause **tooth decay**.

*You need to eat foods containing different things. You should eat lots of some sorts of foods and less of others to have a **balanced diet**.*

The family are eating things from plants and animals. You can show what eats what using a **food chain**. Grandpa's fish comes from the food chain below.

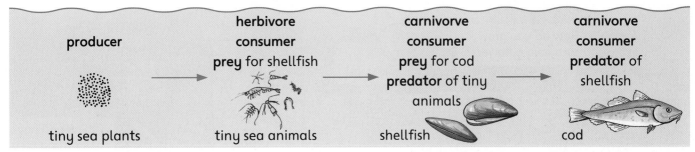

| producer | herbivore consumer **prey** for shellfish | carnivorve consumer **prey** for cod **predator** of tiny animals | carnivorve consumer **predator** of shellfish |
| tiny sea plants | tiny sea animals | shellfish | cod |

*The arrows in a food chain mean 'is eaten by'.*

Some foods are made using **micro-organisms**. For example, Grandma's bread roll is made using **yeast**. Other micro-organisms can make food go off, especially in warm and damp conditions.

*What Grandma's bread roll might look like if it were left in a warm and damp place for a few weeks!*

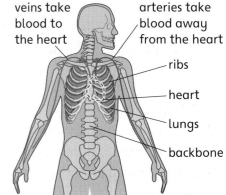

? 6 Copy out the food chain without the drawings. Add Grandpa to your food chain.
7 What is the **prey** of cod?
8 Give two ways in which fish are suited to living under water.

To stay healthy you need to eat the right foods but you also need to exercise. Exercise helps to make your **heart** and **muscles** stronger. When you exercise, your heart beats faster and your **pulse rate** goes up. This is because your heart needs to pump more **blood** (which contains oxygen) around your body to make sure that your muscles get enough blood.

veins take blood to the heart
arteries take blood away from the heart
ribs
heart
lungs
backbone

? 9 What are the tubes that carry blood in your body called? Choose from the following words.

| blood tubes | blood hoses | blood vessels | blood baths |

10 Look at the picture of the family on page 72. Who has the fastest pulse? Explain your answer.
11 List three things your skeleton does for you.
12 a Which **mineral** is needed for healthy teeth and bones?
   b Name a food that contains a lot of this mineral.
   c What life process do you need teeth for?
   d Why should you brush your teeth regularly?

Your skeleton:
• allows you to move because **muscles** move bones at your **joints**.
• supports you, for example your **backbone** supports your body.
• protects important parts of your body, for example your **lungs** are protected by your **ribs**.

73

There are many gardeners who make Adventureworld look pretty. The gardener in the picture is planting **seeds**. These will **germinate** if they have water, warmth and air. They will then grow into plants.

The plants have **flowers** to allow them to **reproduce**. The flowers are **pollinated** by the wind or insects. Once pollinated, a **pollen grain** joins with an **ovum** in a process called **fertilisation** and seeds are formed. Seeds are often found in **fruits**. The fruits **disperse** the seeds using the wind, animals, water or explosions.

**?**

**1** a What do seeds need to germinate?
  b What happens in pollination?
  c How are the plants next to Mum being pollinated?
  d List three ways in which insects can be attracted to plants.
  e Why do you think there are so many wasps around the litter bin?

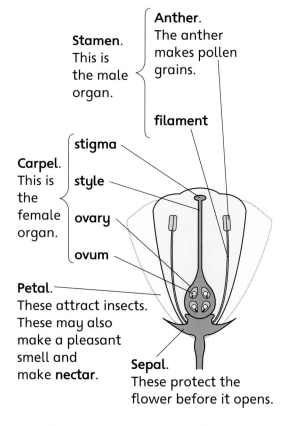

**Stamen**. This is the male organ.

**Anther**. The anther makes pollen grains.

**filament**

**Carpel**. This is the female organ.

stigma
style
ovary
ovum

**Petal**. These attract insects. These may also make a pleasant smell and make **nectar**.

**Sepal**. These protect the flower before it opens.

*The inside of a flower.*

Many seeds are grown in greenhouses, which provide the best conditions for them to germinate and grow into healthy plants.

Plants need air and water, which they use to make new materials in their **leaves**. Plants need light to allow them to make new materials. This is how plants feed! To stay healthy, plants take small amounts of **nutrients** from the soil. Chemical **fertilisers** or **compost** can be added to soils to give plants extra nutrients.

**?**

**2 a** What substances do plants make new materials from? (*Hint*: Light is not a substance.)
 **b** Why do gardeners add fertilisers to their soil?

A plant uses its **roots** to hold it in the soil, and to take water and nutrients out of the soil. It uses its **stem** to carry water and nutrients to other parts of the plant.

*The gardens at Alton Towers.*

*These greenhouses are where the plants are grown for Alton Towers theme park. A team of gardeners work at Alton Towers.*

**?**

**3 a** An **organ** is a part of a living thing that has an important job. Write down the names of four plant organs from the words in bold on these pages.
 **b** What does each organ do?

The gardeners need to know the names of the plants. People use books and **keys** to work out what a plant is called from what it looks like. Plants, just like animals, can be put into groups. For instance, there is a group of plants that lose their leaves in winter and a group of plants that do not.

The gardeners also make sure that there is no litter in the gardens since litter can damage plants and kill animals.

**?**

**4** Look at the picture at the top of page 74. Name two groups you could put all the plants into.

Some of the Smith family are braving a roller coaster! The roller coaster falls downwards because of a **force** called **gravity**. Gravity pulls things towards the centre of the Earth. An upwards force from the track stops the cars falling straight through the track.

The roller coaster cars slow down due to a force called **friction**, which is caused by two surfaces rubbing together. The friction between the track and the wheels slows the cars down, and makes the wheels heat up.

**?**

1 A force is a push or a pull.
   a Does gravity push or pull?
   b Find another push or pull in the picture apart from the roller coaster.
2 Why don't people who live in Australia fall off the bottom of the Earth?

*This doesn't happen!*

Another type of friction, **air resistance**, also slows down the cars. Air resistance is caused by air pushing against things that are moving.

Forces can be measured with a **forcemeter** and are measured in **newtons (N)**. Their directions can be shown with arrows.

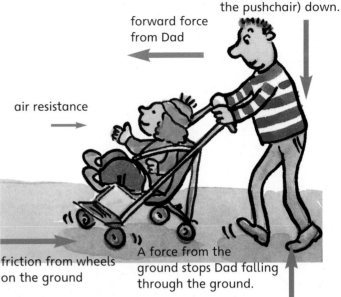

forward force from Dad

Gravity pulls Dad and the pushchair) down.

air resistance

friction from wheels on the ground

A force from the ground stops Dad falling through the ground.

*The different forces on Emma's pushchair.*

**3** The bigger the area of something moving through air, the bigger the air resistance. Which of these will have the biggest air resistance?

| | |
|---|---|
| a roller coaster car | an arrow |
| a parachute | a racing car |

There are lots of lights on around the roller coaster. Things that make light are called **light sources**. Light travels in straight lines from a source, but cannot go through **opaque** things and so **shadows** form.

We can see light sources when light from them travels to our **eyes**. Many things **reflect** light, including this page, but shiny, smooth surfaces reflect light very well. You can see yourself if you look into a shiny, smooth surface such as a mirror.

a light ray

light from the camera flash

*The people on the roller coaster see the light from the camera flash as it travels to their eyes.*

**4 a** Write down two places where there are light sources in the picture.
 **b** How are shadows formed?
**5** Which surfaces reflect light best in the picture at the top of page 76?

There are lots of different **sounds** around the roller coaster which we can hear using our **ears**. Sounds are made by objects when they **vibrate** and the sounds need to travel through a substance such as air.

The more of an object that is vibrating, the lower the **pitch** of the sound. So a thick guitar string makes a lower sound than a thin one, and a long guitar string makes a lower sound than a short one. The harder a string is plucked, the **louder** the sound.

**6** How are sounds made?
**7** How could the man in the picture at the top of page 76 play his drum louder?

# At the orrery

The Smith family are looking at a model of the **planets** (an orrery) at Adventureworld. The model is interesting because the planets seem to float in mid air. This is done using magnets.

Each planet has a magnet inside it and another magnet underneath it. The two magnets repel which means that there is a **magnetic force** pushing them apart.

**?**

**1 a** Magnets have two **poles**, a **north pole** and a **south pole**. Do two north poles **attract** or **repel**?

**b** What would happen if the planet on the diagram were turned upside down?

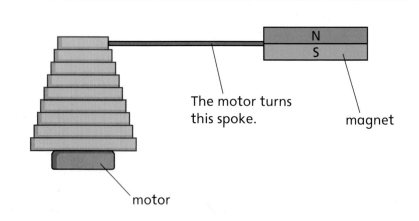

planet

motor

The motor turns this spoke.

magnet

Each magnet under a planet is attached to a spoke on a wheel. The wheels are turned by a **motor**. James is using a **switch** to turn on the motor to make the planets move. The **circuit** is drawn like this.

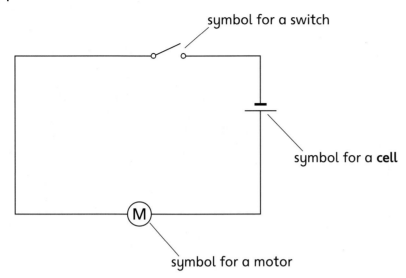

symbol for a switch

symbol for a **cell**

symbol for a motor

The **planets** are all roughly ball-shaped (they are **spheres**) and move around the Sun along paths called **orbits**. The Earth takes one **year** to orbit the Sun. Our Moon takes 28 **days** to go once round the Earth.

As the Earth orbits the Sun, it turns on its **axis**, which is an imaginary line drawn through the Earth. This turning makes the Sun appear to be in different positions during the day, and gives us day and night.

Shadows also change during a day. Look at the shadows of the three sailing boats.

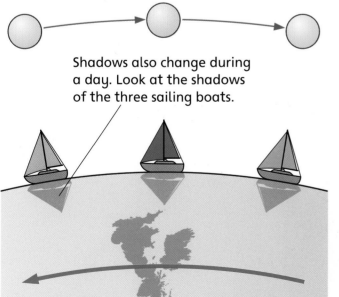

not to scale

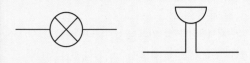

**2** The symbols for a **lamp** and a **buzzer** look like this.

Lamp.                    Buzzer.

   **a** The 'Sun' in the orrery is always shining. Draw a **circuit diagram** to show how the 'Sun' should be connected to a cell.
   **b** How could you change your circuit to make the Sun glow brighter?

**3** How many days does it take for the Earth to go round the Sun?
**4** What shape is the Earth?
**5** Copy this drawing of a stick in the ground and the Sun. It is 8 am in the summer.

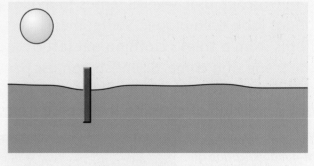

   **a** Draw in the shadow of the stick.
   **b** Draw the Sun and the stick at 12 pm.
   **c** Draw the Sun and the stick at 6 pm.
**6** Why do we get day and night?

*To us it looks as if the Sun is moving across the sky as shown by the blue arrows. However, the Sun appears to move because the Earth is turning (red arrow).*

# Big and small

## How can we see very large and very small things?

Our eyes are very important to us. We use them to help us to find our way around, to help us to do things, and to find out about the world around us.

We can see small things like grains of salt using our eyes, and we can see distant things like the Moon. However, we can see these things in much more detail if we use lenses to help us to see them.

A hand lens is a small magnifying glass. It can make things look bigger, so that we can see more details. Most hand lenses can make things look 10 times bigger than they really are. We say they have a magnification of ×10 (times 10).

*This is what salt crystals look like when you look at them through a hand lens.*

Police detectives sometimes use magnifying glasses to look at evidence left at the scene of a crime. For instance, police might find soil in a stolen car that has fallen off a thief's shoes. If they examine the soil carefully, they may be able to tell which part of the country the thief came from.

A microscope uses several lenses to make things look even bigger. Sometimes fibres from a thief's clothing get left at the scene of a crime. Scientists can use microscopes to look at the fibres, and find out what kind of clothing they came from.

*This is a cotton thread at a magnification of ×60 (right) and ×5 (far right).*

Lenses can also help us to see things that are very far away.
Astronomers use telescopes to investigate the planets and the stars.

This telescope is used for finding out about the planets and stars.

This is the planet Jupiter, as seen through a telescope. We can sometimes see Jupiter without telescopes, but it just looks like a bright star.

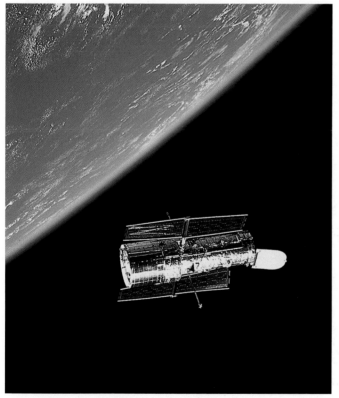

The Hubble Space Telescope is orbiting the Earth. It can take photographs of stars without clouds getting in the way.

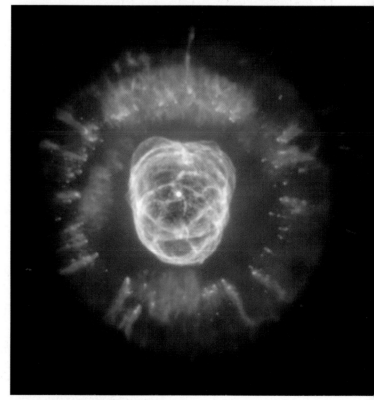

This is a photograph of stars taken with the Hubble Space Telescope. The clouds in the photograph are clouds of space dust.

## P A water-drop lens

The lenses used in microscopes and hand lenses are pieces of glass that are thick in the middle and thin around the edges.

You can make a simple lens using a drop of water.

- What can you see with a water-drop lens?

## P Observing with a hand lens

A hand lens can magnify things by up to 10 times.

You can use a hand lens to investigate lots of different questions.

- What shape are grains of salt, sand or sugar? How big are they?
- What are the differences in cloth used for towels and for shirts?
- How are coloured pictures printed?

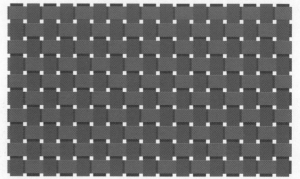

*A piece of cloth, magnified 10 times.*

## P Finding evidence

When a crime is committed, the criminal often leaves clues at the scene of the crime. The clues can be things like soil, fibres from their clothes, or even blood or hair. Scientists can use hand lenses or microscopes to help them to find out if the fibre matches the clothing of a suspect, or if soil matches the soil where the suspect lives.

- Can you identify different kinds of soil?
- Can you describe fibres accurately?

*You can see individual grains of salt in this picture.*

## Pollen

Plants make pollen as part of their life cycle. Each kind of plant has different shaped pollen, so that only the correct kind of pollen can pollinate another flower. Sometimes pollen lands in lakes or bogs, and eventually gets buried. This pollen can last for thousands of years. Scientists can find out about plants that lived in a particular area in the past by digging up pollen from bogs and finding out which plants it comes from.

Find out which plants grow in the school grounds, and what their pollen looks like.

- What would a collection of pollen from a wood look like?

dandelion   horse chestnut

*This is dandelion and horse chestnut pollen.*

## Planets and stars

We live on a planet called the Earth, that orbits the Sun. There are other planets orbiting our Sun, and the Sun is just one of millions of stars. Find out more about the planets and the stars, and make an illustrated report or poster.

- What is the Solar System?
- Find out the names of other planets, and what they are like.
- What is a galaxy?

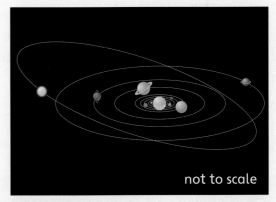

not to scale

*The Solar System.*

## Microscopes and telescopes

Microscopes and telescopes are very important tools for finding out about living things and about space. Find out about the history of microscopes and telescopes.

- Who invented the first ones?
- When were they invented?
- What discoveries have been made using them?
- What do modern scientists use microscopes and telescopes for?

*This is one of the earliest telescopes to be made.*

## How are colours useful?

Many flowers have bright colours. This is because some flowers need insects to carry their pollen from one flower to another, so they can reproduce. Flowers produce a sugary liquid called nectar that insects feed on. Their coloured petals act like a signal, attracting insects to the nectar.

The seeds that plants make need to be dispersed, so the new plants have space to grow properly. Some seeds are inside fruits, and the seeds are dispersed when animals eat the fruits and the seeds get left in their droppings. These fruits are often brightly coloured, so that animals can find them easily.

Some animals use colour to protect themselves from predators, or to help them to catch prey.

*The coloured petals of this flower have attracted the bee.*

*Wild strawberries are red so that birds can see them easily.*

*This owl is camouflaged so that it does not get disturbed while it is sleeping.*

*The patterns in the fur of this tiger help it to hide in the forest while it is waiting to pounce on its prey.*

Some birds have brightly coloured feathers to attract mates. Humans also use colours to attract mates! People have been using make up and dressing in brightly coloured clothes for thousands of years. Today we can buy paints or fabrics in hundreds of different colours. The dyes used in most paints and fabrics are made in chemical reactions in factories. However, these modern dyes have only been available for about 200 years. Before then, people had to use natural materials to colour things around them. Plants, soils and even some animals have all been used to colour things.

Woad is a blue dye made from a plant. The Celts, who lived in England before the Romans invaded, used it to colour their bodies before they fought battles.

We can use colour to find information. The green colour of these bananas tells us that they are not ready to eat.

The numbers on this thermometer change colour according to the temperature.

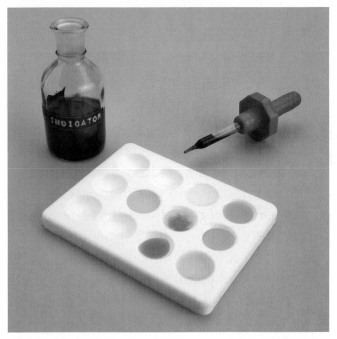

This liquid changes colour when it is put into different kinds of chemical.

## Natural dyes

Before chemical dyes were invented, people used natural materials to dye their clothes.

- Which plants, berries or fruits can be used as dyes?
- How can you get the colour from the plants?
- Which fabrics could you try to dye?
- How will you dye the cloth?

## Indicators

Fizzy drinks, oranges and vinegar all have a sharp taste because they contain chemicals called acids. Other chemicals, such as soap, contain chemicals called alkalis. Some dyes change colour when you put them into an acid or an alkali. A chemical that changes colour like this is called an indicator. Indicators can be made from some plants.

- How can you make an indicator from red cabbage?
- How can you use indicators to find out which foods, drinks or chemicals contain acids or alkalis?

## Chromatography

You have probably mixed paints to get different colours. In the same way, many dyes are made from mixtures of colours. You can find out which colours have been mixed using a process called chromatography.

This chromatogram was made with ink from a black felt pen. It shows that the black ink is a mixture of three different colours.

- Which colours of ink are usually made up of several colours?
- How can you find out if food dyes are a mixture of colours?
- Can you test the dyes used in sweets?

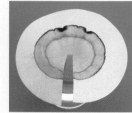

## Coloured animals

Animals are suited (adapted) to the habitat they live in. Some animals are adapted by being camouflaged so that it is difficult for predators to see them. Some predators are camouflaged so that they can creep up on their prey without being seen. Some animals use colour in other ways for protection, and some animals use colour to attract mates.

- How do some animals use colours for camouflage?
- Why do some animals have patterns in their fur?
- Which animals can change their colour?
- How do animals use colour to help them to attract mates?

*A bird of paradise.*

## Flowers

Flowers come in all shapes and colours.

- Why do flowers have such different shapes and colours?
- Do insects see the same colours in flowers as we do?
- Why aren't there many black flowers?
- Why do some plants have small green flowers that insects would not see easily?

## The history of dyes

Modern dyes made in chemical factories have only been available for about 200 years.

- What did people use to make dyes before then?
- Which colours could they make from natural materials?
- Why were colours like purple only worn by rich people?
- How did people make coloured paints?

## How do we measure time?

Time is very important to us. We use the time measured by our watches to make sure we get home in time to watch our favourite programmes on the TV, or when we are arranging to meet someone. We also need to use time to make sure that food is cooked for long enough, and that it does not burn by being cooked for too long!

Thousands of years ago, the time of day did not matter very much. People gathered food or hunted when it was daylight, and went to sleep when it was dark at night. When people started to grow crops, they needed to know when it was the right season for planting seeds. They could measure the time of year by counting days, by counting how many full moons there had been since the last time they planted seeds, or by seeing when the Sun rose or set in a certain place.

*Some of the stones in Stonehenge are arranged so that the Sun rises over them in the middle of winter.*

The Sun rises here in the middle of the summer.

The Sun rises here in the middle of the winter.

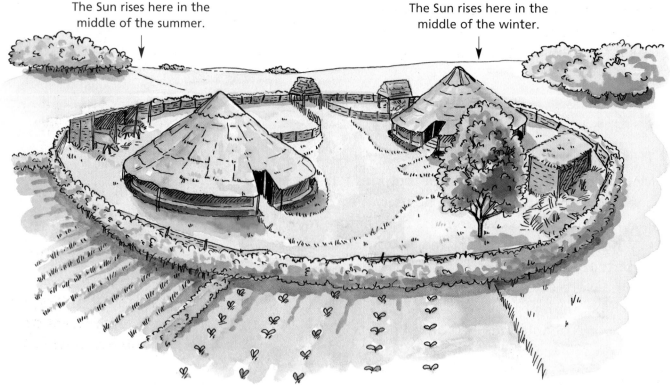

*The Sun rises in different places at different times of the year.*

When people wanted to measure time during the day, they could use sundials. Unfortunately, these are no use at night, or when the Sun isn't shining! People used candles, water clocks or sand clocks to measure the hours in the day.

*This is a simple water clock. Water inside it slowly runs out through a small hole in the bottom. There are marks inside the bowl where you can read the time as the water level drops.*

*We still use sand clocks today for playing games!*

The drawing on the right shows one of the earliest alarm clocks. A Greek teacher called Plato (427–347 BCE) built it to wake his students up in the mornings. Water flowed into container A during the night. When the water level reached the top, it tipped over container B. Lead balls in B hit plate C, and the noise woke up his students!

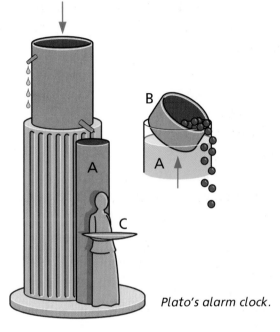

*Plato's alarm clock.*

*The swinging pendulum helps this clock to keep time accurately.*

pendulum

The first mechanical clocks that did not depend on water or sand were made about 700 years ago. However, they were not very accurate. Some of them lost or gained up to 15 minutes each day. Pendulum clocks were invented in the 1650s. Each swing of a pendulum takes the same amount of time, so it can be used to measure regular intervals of time. Pendulum clocks could keep time to within 1 second per day.

Many scientific investigations depend on finding out how long it takes something to happen. Scientists could find out much more about the world when they had accurate clocks.

# Water clocks

Some water clocks work by measuring the level of the water as it drains out of a container. Other clocks work by measuring how long it takes for a container to fill with water.

- How can you build water clocks like these?
- Which type works the best?
- Can you design a water clock to measure 5 minutes?

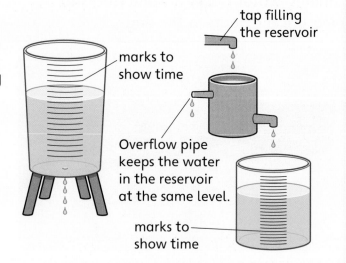

tap filling the reservoir

marks to show time

Overflow pipe keeps the water in the reservoir at the same level.

marks to show time

# Pendulum investigation

A pendulum is a weight on the end of a string that can swing backwards and forwards.

I think that it will swing faster if it has a heavy weight on the end.

A heavy weight will make it swing more slowly.

Do you think the length of the string will make any difference?

It depends on the size of the swing. If it swings a long way, it will take longer.

How can you find out what factors affect the length of time it takes for one swing of the pendulum?

- Which factors could you change?
- How will you make your test fair?
- What will you need to measure?
- Can you predict what you think you will find out?

# The seasons

The weather is very different in summer and winter.

- What causes these differences?
- Do other countries have the same seasons?

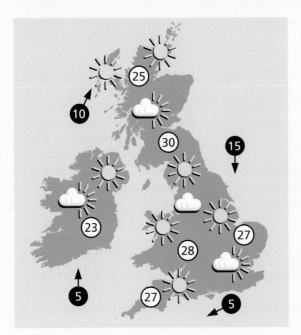
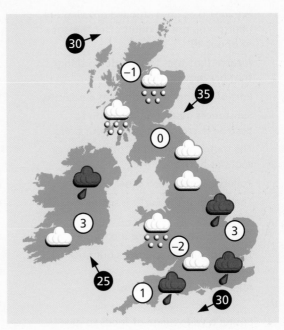

# Life and the seasons

How are plants and animals adapted to the changing seasons?

- Which animals migrate?
- Which animals hibernate?
- How do different trees survive the winter?

# The history of clocks

How did people know the time before clocks were invented?

Find out about the history of clocks, and present your ideas as a timeline or an illustrated report.

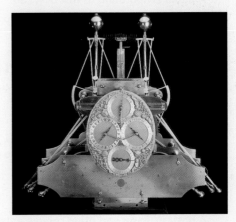

# Glossary

| | |
|---|---|
| adolescence | The time when changes happen to your body and you grow very quickly. This happens when you are a teenager. |
| adult | Humans that have stopped growing are adults. You are an adult after the age of about 19. |
| air resistance | A force that tries to slow down things that are moving through air. |
| alternator | Part of an engine that makes electricity. |
| antibodies | Substances made by your body to destroy micro-organisms in your body. |
| ash | The material that is left after wood or coal has burnt. |
| attract | Pulled towards each other. |
| axis | The line that the Earth is spinning around. |
| babyhood | The time when you are a baby. |
| backbone | The bones running down your back which support you. |
| bacteria (back-*tear*-ree-a) | A kind of micro-organism. |
| balanced diet | Eating a wide range of foods to give you all the food groups you need without having too much of any one food group. |
| balanced forces | Forces that are the same size as each other, and working in opposite directions. |
| bar chart | A chart with columns to show the numbers of things. |
| battery | Part of a circuit that provides the electricity. |
| blood | A red liquid that carries oxygen and food around your body. |
| boiling | A liquid evaporating as fast as it can. |
| bulb | An electrical component that lights up when electricity flows through it. |
| buzzer | An electrical component that makes a noise when electricity flows through it. |
| carbon dioxide | A gas found in the air. It is used in fizzy drinks. It is also absorbed by limewash. |
| carnivore | An animal that eats other animals. |
| cell (*sell*) | A component in a circuit that provides electricity. Several cells together make a battery. |
| childhood | The time between being a baby and being a teenager. |
| circuit (*sir-kit*) | A battery, wires and other components, other components, all joined in a loop. |

| | |
|---|---|
| circuit diagram | A diagram of a circuit that uses symbols. |
| component (com-*po*-nent) | Anything in a circuit. |
| compost | Dead things which have decayed to form a dark brown substance that is put on soil. |
| compost heap | A pile of dead things, like leaves, grass cuttings and vegetable peelings. |
| condensation | A gas changing into a liquid. |
| conduct | Something that allows heat or electricity to go through it is said to conduct heat or electricity. |
| consumer (con-*soo*-mer) | Something in a food chain that eats something else. Animals are consumers. |
| copper | A pinky-brown metal that is used for electrical wiring. |
| day | The time when the Sun lights up the part of the Earth that we are on. |
| decay | When micro-organisms feed on things and turn them into other substances. |
| desalination plant | A factory where distilled water is produced from sea water. |
| disperse | To spread. |
| dissolve | When a solid seems to disappear into a liquid. |
| distillation | When water is evaporated and then condensed to produce pure water. |
| distilled water | Pure water. Water is evaporated and then condensed again. |
| ears | You hear sounds with your ears. |
| electrical conductor (el-*eck*-tri-cal con-*duck*-tor) | A material that lets electricity flow through it. |
| electrical insulator (el-*eck*-tri-cal *ins*-you-lay-ter) | A material that does not let electricity flow through it. |
| electric shock | When electricity flows through your body. |
| electricity | A flow of energy through wires. |
| emulsion | When liquids do not mix together completely. Small droplets of one liquid are formed in the other. |
| evaporate | A liquid turning into a gas. |
| evaporation | A liquid changing into a gas. |
| evidence | Information that helps us to know that something is true. |
| eyes | Light goes into your eyes and allows you to see things. |

| | |
|---|---|
| factor | The thing that you change during an investigation. |
| fair test | An investigation when you only change one factor. |
| feed | Taking in substances to stay alive. For example, animals eat to take in the substances they need. |
| fertilisation (fert-ill-eyes-**ay**-shun) | When the male pollen grain joins with the female ovum (or egg). |
| fertiliser (fert-ill-eyes-er) | Substance that helps plants to grow well. Fertilisers contain nutrients. |
| filter paper | A type of paper with very tiny holes in it that liquids can flow through. You cannot see the holes. |
| filtering | Separating things that have not dissolved in a liquid, by pouring the liquid through a filter such as filter paper. |
| flameproof | Something that does not catch fire very easily. |
| flexible | Things which are flexible are easy to bend. |
| flower | An organ in plants that allows them to reproduce. Flowers produce seeds. |
| force | A push or a pull. |
| forcemeter | A piece of equipment containing a spring that is used to measure forces. |
| friction | A force that tries to slow things down when two things rub together. |
| food chain | A diagram showing who eats who in a food chain. |
| food poisoning | An illness caused by bacteria in food. |
| freeze | Cooling something down until it becomes solid. |
| fruit (**froot**) | Part of a plant, made from a flower, that has seeds. |
| fungi (**fung**-gl or **fung**-gee) | Some of these are big (e.g. mushrooms) and some of these are micro-organisms (e.g. yeast). |
| gas | A substance that can spread all around us. We cannot usually see gases. A gas fills its container, does not keep its volume and will flow. |
| germ (**jerm**) | An everyday word for a micro-organism that causes a disease. |
| germination (jer-min-**ay**-shun) | When a seed starts to grow. |
| gills | Fish have these to allow them to breathe under water. |
| gravity | The force of attraction between two objects. The Earth has a large force of gravity which pulls things towards it. |

| | |
|---|---|
| grow | Getting bigger. |
| gum disease (diz-**zees**) | When bacteria in your mouth cause damage to your gums. |
| habitat | Where something lives (e.g. woodland). |
| hard | Things which are hard are not easily dented. |
| heart | An organ in your body which pumps blood. |
| herbivore | An animal that eats plants. |
| image | The picture that you can see in a mirror. |
| impermeable | A rock that water cannot get into is said to be impermeable. |
| insoluble (in-**sol**-yoo-bull) | Something that does not dissolve. |
| insulator (**ins**-yoo-lay-tor) | Something that does not allow heat or electricity to go through it. |
| irreversible (i-ree-**ver**-sib-bul) | A change where new materials are made. You cannot get the original materials back again. |
| joint | A part of the body where the bones can be moved by muscles. |
| key | A diagram with a list of questions or statements that is used to find out the name of something. |
| lamp | An electrical component that gives out light when electicity goes through it. |
| landfill site | Huge area where rubbish is dumped. |
| leaf | An organ in plants that makes food for the plant using air and water. |
| life processes | Things which all living things do. For example, feed, move, reproduce and grow. |
| light source | Something that makes its own light, like the Sun, a candle or a light bulb. |
| lime | A substance produced when limestone is heated. Also known as quicklime. |
| lime kiln | Lime or quicklime is made in one of these. |
| limestone | A common type of rock which is found in many parts of the UK. |
| limewash | Slaked lime that is used on the outside of houses. |
| line graph | A graph with a line through the points. It is used when the numbers between the values marked on the scale mean something. |
| liquid (**lick**-wid) | A substance that is runny and does not have a fixed shape. A liquid takes up the shape of its container but keeps its volume and will flow. |

| | |
|---|---|
| liquid foam | A liquid which has a gas mixed in with it, but the gas has not dissolved. |
| loud | A loud sound has a high volume. |
| lunar eclipse | When the Earth is between the Sun and the Moon. The Moon is in the shadow of the Earth. |
| magnet | A magnet has two poles, north and south. Two poles of the same type attract each other but a north pole and a south pole will repel each other. Magnets attract magnetic materials. |
| magnetic force | The force from a magnet on another magnet or on a magnetic material. |
| mains electricity | Electricity supplied to houses and schools. It has a high voltage. |
| materials | Everything is made of a material. Different materials are used to make different things. |
| melt | Warming up a solid until it changes into a liquid. |
| metal | Metals are strong and conduct electricity and heat. |
| microbe | Another name for a micro-organism. |
| micro-organism (my-crO-**org**-an-iz-m) | A tiny living thing. |
| microscope | Something that makes tiny things appear much bigger. You can use a microscope to see micro-organisms. |
| mineral | A substance that you need small amounts of in your diet to stay healthy, for example, calcium. |
| mirror | Something very shiny that reflects light very well. You can see images (pictures) of things in mirrors. |
| mixture | When two or more substances are mixed together. |
| motor | A component which spins when electricity flows through it. |
| mould (mold) | A micro-organism which causes things to decay. |
| move | Going from place to place. |
| muscle (**muss**-el) | Part of the body that can contract (get shorter). |
| natural gas | The gas that we burn in cookers or gas fires. |
| newton | The unit of force (N). |
| north pole | The pole of a magnet that points north if the magnet is allowed to spin freely. It will attract a south pole of another magnet but repel another north pole. |
| nutrient (**new**-tree-ent) | Substance found in the soil and in fertiliser that plants need to grow. |

| | |
|---|---|
| old age | People are in old age once they are about 70 years old. |
| opaque (O-**pake**) | Material which does not let light through. |
| orbit | The path that the Earth follows around the Sun. |
| organ | A part of your body or any living thing which has a very important job. |
| ovum (O-vum) | Female part of a plant which joins with a pollen grain in fertilisation. The plural is ova. Also called an egg. |
| partial eclipse | A solar eclipse when only part of the Sun is blocked out. |
| permeable | A rock which water can get into is said to be permeable. |
| pitch | How high or low a sound is. |
| planet | A large object that orbits the Sun. |
| pollen grain | Male part of a plant which joins with an ovum (egg) in fertilisation. |
| pollination (poll-in-**ay**-shun) | When pollen grains land on a stigma. |
| pond dipping | Putting a net into a pond and seeing what small animals you can find. |
| predator | An animal that hunts other animals to eat. |
| prediction (pred-**ick**-shun) | What you think will happen in an experiment. |
| prey | An animal that is hunted by other animals. |
| producer (prod-**you**-ser) | Something in a food chain that can make its own food. Plants are producers. |
| property | What something is like. For example, one property of solids is that they keep their shapes. |
| pulse rate | The number of times you can feel your pulse 'beat' in one minute. |
| pure (p'your) | When a substance is pure there are no other substances mixed with it. |
| quicklime | Produced when limestone is heated. Also known as lime. |
| recharge | When electricity is passed through batteries. |
| reflect | When light bounces off something. |
| repel | Pushed away from each other. |
| reproduce | When living things have young they are said to reproduce. |
| reversible (ree-**ver**-sib-bul) | A change where you can get the original materials back again. |
| ribs | Bones which protect the heart and lungs. |

| | |
|---|---|
| rigid | Things which are rigid do not bend easily. |
| roots | An organ in plants that takes water and nutrients out of the soil. The roots also keep the plant in place. |
| seed | It is made in the flower of a plant and can grow into a new plant. |
| seed dispersal (diss-*per*-sal) | Fruits are used to carry seeds (disperse them) away from where they are made. This can be done by animals, the wind, water or explosions. |
| sieve (siv) | Something that has holes in it so that a liquid will go through the holes but big insoluble things will not. |
| shadow | A place where light cannot get to, because an opaque object is blocking the light. |
| skeleton | The bones inside you. |
| slaked lime | Made by adding water to lime or quicklime. |
| smokejumpers | Men and women who parachute out of an aeroplane to a place near a fire to help to put it out. |
| solar cells | These make electricity when the Sun shines on them. |
| solar eclipse | When the Moon is between the Sun and the Earth. The Moon casts a shadow on part of the Earth. |
| solid | A solid keeps its shape and its volume, will not flow and is usually hard. |
| soluble (*sol*-yoo-bull) | Something that dissolves. |
| solution (sol-*oo*-shun) | A liquid that has a substance dissolved in it. |
| sounds | Sounds are made when things vibrate. Sounds travel through things. |
| south pole | The pole of a magnet that points south if the magnet is allowed to spin freely. It will attract a north pole of another magnet but repel another south pole. |
| sphere (s'*fear*) | A round shape, like a football. |
| states of matter | There are three forms or states of matter – solid, liquid and gas. |
| stationary (*stay*-shun-ry) | Not moving. |
| stem | An organ in plants that supports the plant. |
| strong | Things which are strong do not break easily. |
| switch | A component which can make a gap in a circuit, to turn other components on or off. |

| | |
|---|---|
| symbol (sim-bol) | A way of representing something by a simple sign or drawing. |
| teenage | Humans that are between 13 and 19 years old. |
| thaw | Letting something warm up until it melts (turns from a solid into a liquid). |
| tooth decay | When bacteria in your mouth cause holes to form in your teeth. |
| total eclipse | A solar eclipse when the Sun is completely blocked out by the Moon. |
| translucent (trans-*loo*-sent) | Material through which a glow of light can be seen. |
| transparent | Material which light can travel through. |
| unbalanced forces | When two forces working in opposite directions are not the same strength. |
| upthrust | A force from water that pushes things up. |
| vaccination | An injection that stops you getting a particular disease. |
| vaccine | Contains dead or weak micro-organisms that cause a particular disease, used to stop you getting that disease. |
| vibrate (v-eye-*brate*) | Move backwards and forwards. |
| virus (vy-rus) | A kind of micro-organism. |
| vitamin | A substance that you need small amounts of in your diet to stay healthy, for example, vitamin C. |
| voltage | A way of saying how powerful electricity is. |
| volume | The amount of space something takes up. |
| water cycle | Water evaporates from the sea, condenses to form clouds, falls as rain, and eventually runs back to the sea again. |
| water vapour (*war*-ter *vay*-per) | Another name for water when it is a gas. |
| weight | The amount of force on something from gravity. It is measured in newtons. |
| wind turbine | This makes electricity when the wind blows. |
| year | The time it takes for the Earth to go around the Sun once. A year lasts $365\frac{1}{4}$ days. |
| yeast | A kind of micro-organism used to make bread. |

# Index